T0381106

Terraform Made Easy

Provisioning, Managing and Automating Cloud Infrastructure with Terraform on Google Cloud

Ivy Wang

Apress®

Terraform Made Easy: Provisioning, Managing and Automating Cloud Infrastructure with Terraform on Google Cloud

Ivy Wang
Herzogenaurach, Germany

ISBN-13 (pbk): 979-8-8688-1009-1
https://doi.org/10.1007/979-8-8688-1010-7

ISBN-13 (electronic): 979-8-8688-1010-7

Managing Director, Apress Media LLC: Welmoed Spahr
Acquisitions Editor: James Robinson-Prior
Development Editor: James Markham
Editorial Assistant: Gryffin Winkler

Cover designed by eStudioCalamar

Cover image designed by SerenityArt from Pixabay (https://pixabay.com/)

Distributed to the book trade worldwide by Springer Science+Business Media New York, 1 New York Plaza, Suite 4600, New York, NY 10004-1562, USA. Phone 1-800-SPRINGER, fax (201) 348-4505, e-mail orders-ny@springer-sbm.com, or visit www.springeronline.com. Apress Media, LLC is a California LLC and the sole member (owner) is Springer Science + Business Media Finance Inc (SSBM Finance Inc). SSBM Finance Inc is a **Delaware** corporation.

For information on translations, please e-mail booktranslations@springernature.com; for reprint, paperback, or audio rights, please e-mail bookpermissions@springernature.com.

Apress titles may be purchased in bulk for academic, corporate, or promotional use. eBook versions and licenses are also available for most titles. For more information, reference our Print and eBook Bulk Sales web page at http://www.apress.com/bulk-sales.

Any source code or other supplementary material referenced by the author in this book is available to readers on GitHub (https://github.com/Apress). For more detailed information, please visit https://www.apress.com/gp/services/source-code.

If disposing of this product, please recycle the paper

Table of Contents

About the Author

Ivy Wang is a distinguished data scientist and cloud architect, celebrated for her deep expertise and impactful contributions to the tech industry. As an honored Google Women Techmakers Ambassador, Ivy's leadership and dedication to advancing technology have earned her widespread recognition.

With a passion for innovation, Ivy excels in simplifying complex systems and automating processes in big data and AI projects. Her ability to turn intricate challenges into streamlined, efficient solutions consistently drives enhanced performance and operational excellence.

About the Technical Reviewers

Scott Winkler is the author of "Terraform in Action" and a former lead engineer of Snowflake's Terraform provider. He has spoken about Terraform at conferences such as HashiConf, HashiTalks, and Snowflake Summit and is a 2020 recipient of HashiCorp's Ambassador and Core Contributor awards.

Kerim Satirli is a senior developer advocate at HashiCorp, where he coaches operators and developers on sustainable infrastructure and orchestration workflows.

Before he joined HashiCorp, Kerim worked on Industrial IoT for the Amsterdam airport and helped museums bring more of their collections online.

When Kerim isn't working, he's either spending time with his daughter, enjoying aerial photography, or baking a cake.

Acknowledgments

Writing this book has been an extraordinary journey, filled with both profound challenges and personal growth. As I navigated these trials, I found strength and resilience, and I am deeply grateful to the many individuals and organizations that supported and inspired me along the way.

First, I extend my heartfelt thanks to Scott Winkler and Kerim Satirli. Your guidance and insightful suggestions were truly invaluable. As prominent figures in the industry, your enthusiasm and meticulous attention to detail were both inspiring and reassuring. Even during moments when I struggled with impatience, your thoughtful review of every line of code and your constructive feedback meant a great deal to me.

I also want to express my profound appreciation to Anuj Tyagi, an experienced infrastructure architect, and Harshavardhan Nerella, a seasoned cloud engineer and Kubernetes expert. Your professional feedback, review of drafts, and insights into industry solutions were crucial in shaping the book's content. Your expertise helped me refine and enhance the material significantly.

To my family and friends, thank you for your unwavering patience, understanding, and encouragement throughout this endeavor. Your support has been a source of strength, and I couldn't have completed this project without you.

ACKNOWLEDGMENTS

Finally, a sincere thank-you to Apress and Springer Nature, and especially to James Robinson-Prior, Gryffin Winkler, Krishnan Sathyamurthy, and James Markham. Your assistance made the writing process smoother and more enjoyable. Your professionalism and dedication were instrumental in bringing this book to fruition.

This book is a collective achievement, and I am deeply appreciative of everyone who contributed to its creation. Thank you all for being an integral part of this journey.

Preface

Reflecting on my journey through the ever-evolving world of data science, I've had the opportunity to lead and contribute to various machine learning (ML) and artificial intelligence (AI) projects. These experiences have sharpened my technical skills and highlighted a significant gap in our ecosystem: the need for a more organized and traceable approach to infrastructure management.

The concept of infrastructure as code (IaC) and the advent of Terraform immediately captured my interest. IaC's philosophy aligns with my approach—rather than managing countless lines of code to detail every aspect, you define the desired state of your resources and let Terraform, in conjunction with the platform, handle the rest. Terraform's lightweight nature and its integration with more than 1,000 providers make it a versatile tool, regardless of the cloud platform your organization uses.

Terraform has genuinely transformed my approach to infrastructure management. It has alleviated the repetitive tasks of daily operations and significantly reduced the risk of human error. While mistakes are an inevitable part of being human, IaC and Terraform enhance our processes, making them more transparent, traceable, and reliable. Just like the book's title suggests, Terraform has indeed made a lot of things easier!

This realization inspired me to explore Terraform deeply and share my experiences through this book. I wholeheartedly recommend it to data engineers, data scientists, machine learning engineers, and solution architects. It's not just a tool for efficiency; it's a way to refine your workflow and maintain your peace of mind in a demanding field.

What You'll Gain from This Book

Welcome to your comprehensive guide to mastering Terraform—the leading tool for IaC. Whether you're just starting out or looking to enhance your existing cloud management skills, this book is designed to elevate your understanding and application of Terraform.

Here's what you can expect from this resource:

- **A Strong Foundation:** We begin by simplifying IaC and Terraform, clarifying their benefits for efficiency, collaboration, and consistency in infrastructure management. You'll grasp the core reasons behind adopting IaC and how it can transform your approach to managing infrastructure.

- **Practical, Hands-on Learning:** Engage with practical exercises right from the start. We'll walk you through the installation of Terraform and teach you the essential commands—init, plan, apply, and destroy. With these skills, you'll confidently manage your infrastructure using code.

- **Harnessing Terraform's Full Potential:** We'll explore the fundamental concepts that make Terraform so effective. You'll become adept with providers, variables, modules, and dependencies—key elements for creating efficient, reusable infrastructure configurations.

- **Real-World Applications:** Dive into Chapter 4 for hands-on examples that demonstrate Terraform's capabilities. You'll learn to provision crucial Google Cloud Platform (GCP) components—from compute engines and virtual networks to cloud storage, databases, backups, and Kubernetes clusters.

- **Advanced Infrastructure Management:** Infrastructure management goes beyond just deployment. In Chapter 5, we focus on critical aspects such as security and performance. Explore secrets management, state management, disaster recovery, and tools like Secret Manager, Identity and Access Management (IAM), and Role-Based Access Control (RBAC).

- **Collaboration and Automation:** Effective management thrives on teamwork and automation. The final chapter covers how to collaborate efficiently, integrate testing to boost performance, and automate your infrastructure processes. We also provide best practices and industry insights to enhance your IaC expertise.

This book isn't just about commands and examples—it's a thorough guide that will help you understand IaC and Terraform deeply, apply these concepts effectively, and build secure, scalable, and efficient cloud infrastructure.

How to Use This Book

This guide is crafted to be a flexible learning tool tailored to your needs, regardless of your experience level. Here's how to navigate it based on your background:

- **For Beginners in Cloud and IaC (Chapters 1--3):** Start with the basics in Chapter 1, which introduces IaC and its advantages. You'll see how IaC improves efficiency, repeatability, and collaboration in infrastructure management. Chapters 2 and 3 build your practical skills with Terraform, teaching you installation and key commands. These chapters will give you the confidence to manage infrastructure through code.

- **For Experienced Terraform Users Seeking GCP Expertise (Chapter 4):** If you're already familiar with Terraform, jump to Chapter 4. This chapter features 18 detailed examples of provisioning essential GCP components, from compute engines and networks to storage and Kubernetes clusters.

- **For Advanced Users: Enhancing Security, Performance, and Automation (Chapters 5 and 6):** If you have a solid grasp of Terraform and want to advance further, Chapters 5 and 6 are for you. Chapter 5 covers security and performance topics, including secrets management, state management, and disaster recovery. Chapter 6 focuses on optimization and collaboration, exploring testing, automation, and best practices to streamline your workflows and enhance team productivity.

- **Learning at Your Own Pace:** Feel free to move around the chapters based on your current knowledge and interests. For those new to cloud and IaC, following the chapters sequentially will provide a comprehensive learning experience.

The following are additional tips for success:

- **Experiment:** Hands-on practice is crucial. Don't hesitate to try the examples and explore beyond the basics.

- **Practice Regularly:** Frequent use of Terraform will build your comfort and expertise. Personal projects or real-world scenarios are excellent for practice.

- **Utilize Online Resources:** The tech community is rich with resources. Use forums, tutorials, and documentation to deepen your understanding and tackle specific questions.

By following these guidelines and leveraging the structured learning paths in this book, you'll be well on your way to mastering Terraform and managing your GCP infrastructure with confidence.

CHAPTER 1

Introduction to IaC and Terraform

If I have to sum up why learning Terraform is worth it in one sentence, I'd say it automates and manages your cloud infrastructure efficiently, saving you from tedious, repetitive tasks while ensuring consistency, security, and scalability.

The Traditional Approach of Managing Infrastructure Resources

Before we dive into the nuances of infrastructure as code (IaC), let's take a moment to reflect on the era of manual infrastructure management. Maya Angelou once said, "I have great respect for the past. If you don't know where you've come from, you don't know where you're going." By exploring the challenges of traditional methods, we can truly appreciate the transformative impact of modern IaC solutions.

Imagine you're a data scientist at a cutting-edge e-commerce company that's fully integrated with cloud technology, particularly the Google Cloud Platform (GCP). Your current task is to set up a new compute instance for a machine learning project. How would you approach this?

© Ivy Wang 2024
I. Wang, *Terraform Made Easy*, https://doi.org/10.1007/979-8-8688-1010-7_1

Initially, you might consider using an intuitive graphical user interface (GUI)—a tool that simplifies the creation of virtual machines with just a few clicks. Alternatively, if you're more inclined toward coding, the command-line interface (CLI) offers a quicker, more precise option preferred by tech enthusiasts. For instance, you could use a command to swiftly spin up your compute instance, streamlining the process with efficiency and precision.

Option1: Creating a Virtual Machine with a GUI

Figure 1-1. *Creating a Virtual Machine Using the Graphical User Interface (GUI)*

Option 2: Creating a Virtual Machine with the CLI

```
ivyvan_w@cloudshell:~ (terraform-made-easy)$ gcloud compute
instances create instance-example \
    --image-family debian-11 \
    --image-project debian-cloud \
    --machine-type e2-medium \
    --subnet default \
    --zone europe-west3-a
```

The Growing Complexity of Managing Infrastructure

Managing a small number of resources is straightforward, but scaling up brings a whole new set of challenges. For example, imagine managing 400 virtual machines spread across 3 regions and 8 departments. Traditional methods simply can't keep up with this level of complexity.

Manually provisioning resources is slow and prone to errors. With so many machines, typos, misconfigurations, and missed details are inevitable. This isn't about carelessness—it's just the reality of managing large-scale operations by hand. To minimize mistakes and speed up the process, a more advanced approach is essential.

Resource management becomes even more challenging when you have to maintain hundreds of virtual machines across different stages— development, testing, staging, and production. It's like trying to manage a group of fast-moving kittens: difficult to keep track of and prone to slipping through the cracks. This problem worsens when changes happen and documentation doesn't keep pace, leaving you without a clear record.

The challenges of managing infrastructure go far beyond just virtual machines. As you add more elements such as storage, databases, networks, and Kubernetes, the complexity multiplies. Here are some common challenges that businesses face when managing large-scale environments:

- **Time-Consuming Processes**

  Provisioning multiple servers manually is inherently slow. Each resource has to be configured individually, causing significant delays in project timelines. As the demand for faster deployment grows, relying on manual methods can hold back progress and lead to missed deadlines.

- **Error-Prone Configurations**

  Manual configurations are vulnerable to human error.
  Even a small mistake in setting up a server or a network
  can lead to major issues, compromising the security,
  performance, and stability of the entire system. These
  errors can be difficult to trace, and fixing them often
  requires significant time and resources.

- **Inconsistent Setups**

  When each server is manually configured, ensuring
  consistency across the infrastructure becomes a
  real challenge. Small differences in setup can lead
  to operational discrepancies, which might cause
  failures or performance issues. Maintaining uniform
  configurations across a growing environment becomes
  increasingly difficult without a standardized approach.

- **Increased Complexity in Manual Configurations**

  As the network architecture becomes more intricate,
  managing it manually becomes unsustainable. The
  more moving parts there are, the higher the chance for
  errors. Networks, databases, and systems become more
  complex over time, and manual configurations just
  can't keep up with the scale or sophistication required.

- **Insufficient Documentation**

  Changes made through graphical user interfaces
  (GUIs) often lack proper documentation. Without
  clear records of what was changed, it's difficult to
  understand or replicate configurations later. This
  lack of traceability makes troubleshooting and future
  planning much harder.

- **Scaling Challenges**

  Scaling infrastructure to meet increasing demand, whether it's handling more traffic or adding new components, often requires manual adjustments. This approach is inefficient, prone to error, and slow, which hampers the ability to respond to business needs quickly. The manual scaling process simply can't keep up with the fast pace of modern operations.

- **Dependency on Key Individuals**

  Traditional deployment processes often depend on a few individuals with deep knowledge of the infrastructure. This creates a single point of failure—if these individuals are unavailable, the system might become unmanageable. Relying on human expertise without automation leads to operational risks.

- **Limited Rollback Options**

  Without standardized version control systems, rolling back changes becomes a challenging task. If something goes wrong, reversing configurations is difficult, which can delay troubleshooting and resolution. This lack of rollback flexibility increases the risk of long-term disruptions and service downtime.

- **Communication Gaps**

  When teams work in silos without proper collaboration tools or version control systems, communication breaks down. This can lead to conflicting changes, mistakes, and disruptions to the system. A lack of transparency makes it harder to align teams, creating inefficiencies and errors that can affect performance.

5

- **Audibility Challenges**

  Tracking the origin, timing, and reasons behind specific changes is critical for security, compliance, and troubleshooting. However, with manual processes, auditing changes is cumbersome. This makes it difficult to maintain an accurate and accessible record of changes, further complicating problem-solving and governance.

- **Risk of Data Loss**

  Manual changes—especially those made without proper backups—pose a significant risk to data integrity. Accidental deletions or misconfigurations can lead to data loss or corruption, and without a reliable backup and recovery system, restoring the system can be a complex and lengthy process.

The Need for Change: Adopt Infrastructure as Code

The traditional approach to managing infrastructure worked well in simpler times, but as demands grew, its limitations became more apparent. The challenges we've discussed—manual errors, inconsistent setups, and slow scaling—highlight the need for a better way. The solution is clear: businesses need a smarter, automated, and error-resistant method that not only addresses these challenges but also empowers teams to scale efficiently, maintain consistency, and ensure strong operational practices.

This is where *infrastructure as code* comes in. IaC offers a revolutionary approach to managing infrastructure in today's fast-paced, complex IT environments. By treating infrastructure as software—using code to define and manage it—teams can automate provisioning, reduce human errors, and make scaling effortless. IaC allows for version control, consistent setups, and easy rollback, providing the reliability and efficiency that traditional methods simply can't deliver.

In short, adopting IaC is the key to overcoming the limitations of manual management and achieving the agility and consistency required for modern businesses to thrive.

Infrastructure as Code

IaC is a modern approach to managing and provisioning computing infrastructure using machine-readable definition files, instead of manually configuring physical hardware or relying on traditional tools. This method enables developers and system administrators to automate the setup and management of critical resources such as virtual machines, networks, and storage.

Imagine managing an entire data center without ever having to physically touch a server or manually adjust network settings. That's the transformative power of IaC. It revolutionizes infrastructure management by turning a labor-intensive, error-prone task into a streamlined, automated process. Instead of manually configuring infrastructure, you define and manage it through code.

Infrastructure as Code

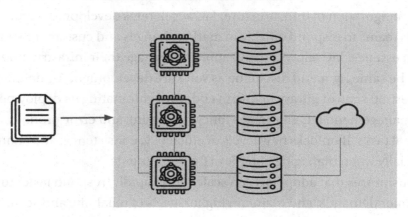

Figure 1-2. *Overview of Infrastructure as Code (IaC)*

Let's look at the example of a retail business running an e-commerce platform. In the past, scaling infrastructure to handle high traffic during peak shopping seasons like Black Friday might have taken weeks, requiring physical server installations, network setups, and storage configurations. With IaC, this process is dramatically simplified. The infrastructure needed to handle the traffic surge is written as code, tested in advance, and can be automatically deployed in minutes, as demand increases.

IaC allows you to define infrastructure using code, often in a specialized language like Terraform or a general-purpose programming language like Python. These code definitions can be stored in version control systems, tested for correctness, and deployed consistently across different environments, just like application code. This ensures that your infrastructure remains in the desired state, with any changes easily reversible, minimizing human error and configuration drift.

In modern DevOps practices, IaC is key to improving collaboration between development and operations teams. For example, a financial services company launching a new online banking feature can use IaC to ensure that both the development and production environments are identical. This eliminates the common issue of "it works on my machine" and enables faster, more reliable releases. By automating the provisioning and configuration of infrastructure, IaC accelerates development and allows teams to respond quickly to market changes and customer needs.

In essence, IaC allows organizations to manage their infrastructure with the same rigor and discipline as software development. By defining the desired state of infrastructure in code and automating its deployment and management, IaC eliminates time-consuming and error-prone manual tasks. It unlocks new levels of efficiency, consistency, and control, especially when managing complex IT environments.

Businesses that adopt IaC can scale more rapidly, respond faster to customer demands, and maintain higher levels of reliability and security. With IaC, teams can focus on delivering value, rather than being bogged down by infrastructure management.

Benefits of Infrastructure as Code

IaC transforms the way we manage and provision infrastructure by using machine-readable configuration files instead of manually configuring physical hardware or relying on traditional tools. Here are the key benefits of adopting IaC, which can significantly modernize infrastructure management and improve operational efficiency.

- **Automate Everything, from Setup to Scaling**

  In the past, setting up IT infrastructure was a time-consuming and error-prone process, involving manual configuration of servers, networks, and storage solutions. With IaC, you can automate this entire process. Instead of spending hours on configurations, you simply define your desired infrastructure state in code, and IaC tools take care of the rest—creating, configuring, and scaling resources automatically.

  For example, imagine an e-commerce company needing to deploy hundreds of servers for a holiday sale. Manually configuring each server would take hours and might lead to mistakes that cause service disruptions. With IaC, a single script can automatically configure all the servers in minutes, ensuring everything is set up correctly and minimizing the risk of downtime during peak periods.

- **Ensure Consistency Across All Environments**

  In modern software development, it's crucial to maintain consistency across development, testing, and production environments to avoid bugs and deployment failures. IaC makes this easy by allowing you to use the same scripts across all environments. This ensures that the infrastructure in development, testing, and production is identical, so developers can confidently test their code, knowing it will work the same way in production.

For instance, a financial services company deploying a new trading app can use IaC to ensure that the development, testing, and production environments are exact matches. This reduces the risk of errors during deployment and ensures smooth, reliable operations across the board.

- **Version Control: Track and Manage Changes**

  Just as software developers use version control to track code changes, IaC enables IT teams to version-control their infrastructure configurations. This is important for tracking changes, identifying issues, and rolling back to previous versions if necessary.

  For example, if a global retail company experiences an issue with its cloud infrastructure after an update, the IT team can quickly review the version history of the infrastructure code to pinpoint the cause of the problem. With IaC, they can revert to a previous, stable configuration, minimizing downtime and ensuring smooth business operations.

- **Simplify Complex Configurations**

  Modern IT infrastructures are often complex, involving many interconnected components. IaC simplifies this complexity by allowing IT teams to define even the most intricate configurations in a clear, readable, and human-friendly format. This makes infrastructure easier to manage, adapt, and scale as the business grows.

For example, a multinational company with a complex cloud infrastructure spanning multiple regions and integrating with various third-party services can use IaC to define and manage their infrastructure in an organized, structured way. This approach makes it easier to scale as the business expands into new markets, allowing the IT team to focus on strategic tasks rather than dealing with day-to-day management.

While Infrastructure as Code simplifies and streamlines infrastructure management, mastering it requires a solid understanding and careful judgment—skills you'll develop as you dive deeper into IaC tools like Terraform. In the next section, we'll explore Terraform's features and how it fits into the IaC landscape.

A Closer Look at Terraform

Terraform, developed by HashiCorp, is a leading IaC tool that has transformed how organizations define, deploy, and manage IT infrastructure. In today's fast-paced business world, where infrastructure must be scalable, reliable, and adaptable, Terraform provides a powerful and flexible solution. It automates infrastructure management, ensuring consistency, repeatability, and efficiency.

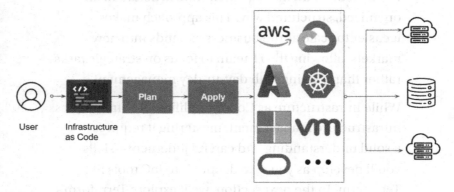

Figure 1-3. *How Terraform Operates: A High-Level Overview*

At its core, Terraform allows users to define their infrastructure using declarative configuration files, written in HashiCorp Configuration Language (HCL) or JavaScript Object Notation (JSON). These configuration files act as a blueprint for your infrastructure, covering everything from virtual machines and storage systems to networking configurations and software-as-a-service (SaaS) integrations. These blueprints are versioned, shared, and reusable, making collaboration easier and ensuring that infrastructure changes are properly tracked and auditable.

Terraform doesn't just define infrastructure—it actively manages its lifecycle, from creation to decommissioning. When you run Terraform, it generates an execution plan that details the steps required to achieve your infrastructure's desired state. Terraform then executes the plan, interacting with various cloud providers and application programming interfaces (APIs) to provision resources as specified.

As your infrastructure evolves, Terraform can automatically detect changes in your configuration files and generate incremental plans that apply only the necessary updates. This avoids the risks and inefficiencies of manual adjustments, ensuring that changes are applied accurately and efficiently—whether you're scaling up resources, migrating between cloud providers, or setting up complex networks.

Key Features of Terraform

Terraform is a robust and flexible tool that simplifies infrastructure management. It allows teams to define, provision, and manage infrastructure across multiple cloud providers and services in a consistent and automated way. Whether managing multicloud environments or complex setups, Terraform provides the scalability and reliability needed to meet modern infrastructure demands.

- **Infrastructure as Code**

  Terraform follows the IaC approach, treating infrastructure like software. This means you can write, test, and version infrastructure configurations just like you would with application code. The benefits of this approach include consistency, automation, and the ability to easily replicate environments from development to production.

- **Execution Plans**

  Before making any changes, Terraform generates an execution plan that shows exactly what will be created, modified, or destroyed in your infrastructure. This step-by-step plan provides clarity and ensures that changes are predictable and safe, minimizing the risk of unexpected issues.

- **State Management**

  Terraform's state management is essential for keeping an accurate representation of your infrastructure. It tracks the current state of your resources, allowing Terraform to determine what changes are needed to reach the desired state. This persistent state can be stored locally or remotely, keeping your infrastructure synchronized and preventing configuration drift.

- **Change Automation**

  Terraform automates complex infrastructure changes, applying them in the correct order with minimal human intervention. This automation reduces the chances of errors, increases reliability, and frees your team to focus on higher-level tasks rather than managing manual configurations.

- **Provider Ecosystem**

  One of Terraform's strengths is its provider ecosystem, which includes hundreds of providers. Providers interact with cloud platform APIs and other services, allowing Terraform to manage resources across various environments. This makes it possible to manage cloud services, on-premises infrastructure, and third-party tools—all in a single workflow.

Benefits of Terraform

In today's complex and rapidly changing IT environments, managing infrastructure manually is not only tedious but also prone to errors. Modern infrastructures often span multiple cloud platforms, regions, and service types, making manual management increasingly difficult.

Terraform provides a solution by offering a unified and consistent approach to infrastructure management, whether it's in the cloud, on-premises, or in a hybrid setup.

- **Declarative Syntax**

  One of the core strengths of Terraform is its declarative syntax. With Terraform, you simply define the desired state of your infrastructure—what you want to have in place—without needing to specify the step-by-step process for achieving it. Terraform handles the implementation details, streamlining the management of infrastructure and allowing teams to focus on the desired outcome, not the process.

- **Human-Readable Configuration**

  Terraform uses HCL, a configuration language designed to be easy to read and write, even for those with limited programming experience. This human-readable format promotes collaboration among team members and makes maintaining infrastructure code easier. It ensures that infrastructure configurations are accessible to a wide range of stakeholders, from developers to operations teams.

- **State Management**

  Terraform tracks your infrastructure's current state with a state file. This helps ensure that the infrastructure remains consistent with the desired configuration, even as changes are made. By maintaining this up-to-date state, Terraform can apply precise updates and prevent infrastructure drift, where manual changes lead to inconsistencies and potential issues over time.

- **Version Control Integration**

  Terraform integrates seamlessly with version control systems like Git. This integration enables teams to track changes over time, collaborate effectively, and revert to previous versions if needed. It supports best practices in infrastructure management, such as continuous integration (CI) and automated testing, ensuring that any changes to infrastructure are well-managed and auditable.

- **Multicloud Management**

  Terraform allows for seamless management of infrastructure across multiple cloud platforms like AWS, Azure, and Google Cloud. This capability helps organizations avoid being locked into a single provider, giving them the flexibility to choose the best services for their needs. It also enables businesses to optimize costs by taking advantage of the different pricing structures and features offered by each provider.

- **Community and Extensibility**

  Terraform benefits from a large, active community and a rich ecosystem of prebuilt modules and providers. The Terraform Registry offers a wide range of resources to extend Terraform's capabilities, allowing users to quickly add new functionalities or integrate with different services. This extensive ecosystem helps organizations save time and effort, enabling them to meet a variety of infrastructure needs with minimal custom work.

Summary

In this chapter, you explored Terraform—a powerful tool designed to simplify and automate the management of cloud infrastructure. We covered key concepts such as declarative syntax, state management, and the extensive provider ecosystem that makes Terraform highly versatile.

- **Declarative Syntax**: You now understand how Terraform's declarative language allows you to define the desired state of your infrastructure, enabling Terraform to automatically implement the necessary changes.

- **State Management**: You discovered how Terraform tracks and manages the state of your infrastructure, ensuring consistency and reproducibility across deployments.

- **Provider Ecosystem**: You explored the broad range of providers available for Terraform, allowing you to manage infrastructure across multiple cloud platforms and services.

Terraform is crucial for modern infrastructure management because it:

- **Simplifies Complex Tasks**: Automates the provisioning and management of infrastructure, saving time and effort.

- **Ensures Consistency**: Maintains a consistent state for your infrastructure, reducing errors and enhancing reliability.

- **Supports Multiple Clouds**: Works seamlessly across various cloud platforms, offering flexibility and choice.

As you continue reading, you'll discover practical applications of Terraform in various scenarios, from automating infrastructure tasks to managing multicloud environments. By the end of this book, you'll be equipped with the skills to harness the full power of Terraform and elevate your infrastructure management to new heights.

CHAPTER 2

Getting Started with Terraform

Before we dive into the specifics of Terraform, let me share a story about Marlon, a seasoned machine learning engineer. Marlon was deeply passionate about data, algorithms, and refining models to uncover insights. His days were filled with working on complex machine learning tasks, but he found himself spending too much time managing infrastructure—provisioning virtual machines, configuring networks, and scaling resources. These repetitive, manual tasks were eating into the time he truly wanted to dedicate to his core work.

That's when Marlon discovered Terraform. This tool promised to simplify and automate infrastructure management with a simple, declarative language. Intrigued by the idea, Marlon decided to give it a try. He was immediately impressed by how easy it was to define and manage his infrastructure using just a few lines of code. Terraform handled the mundane tasks—provisioning virtual machines, setting up networks, and scaling resources—allowing Marlon to focus on what mattered most.

With Terraform seamlessly integrated into his workflow, Marlon experienced a major boost in efficiency. No longer burdened by infrastructure tasks, he could focus on developing innovative machine learning models, delivering more reliable and cutting-edge solutions. Terraform quickly became his secret weapon for scaling his work, enabling him to move faster and more confidently.

© Ivy Wang 2024
I. Wang, *Terraform Made Easy*, https://doi.org/10.1007/979-8-8688-1010-7_2

Marlon's experience is a great example of how Terraform can transform your workflow. Whether you're a developer, system administrator, or cloud architect, Terraform helps automate infrastructure management, freeing you from repetitive tasks and empowering you to focus on what you do best.

In this chapter, walk you through the essential steps to get started with Terraform. Here's what we'll cover:

- **Installation**

  We'll begin by guiding you through the process of installing Terraform on your preferred operating system. Whether you're working on Windows, macOS, or Linux, we'll make sure you get Terraform up and running smoothly.

- **Configuration Language**

  Next, we'll dive into the simple yet powerful configuration language Terraform uses to define infrastructure. You'll learn the basics of HashiCorp Configuration Language (HCL), which is intuitive and human-readable, making it easy for you to describe the infrastructure you need with just a few lines of code.

- **Basic Commands**

  After you're familiar with the configuration language, we'll introduce you to the most commonly used Terraform commands, such as `init`, `plan`, and `apply`. You'll understand how to initialize your working directory, generate execution plans, and apply changes to your infrastructure.

By the end of this chapter, you'll be equipped with the foundational knowledge to use Terraform effectively. You'll feel confident in your ability to automate basic infrastructure management tasks so you are ready to dive into more advanced concepts and real-world applications in later chapters.

Terraform Installation

Terraform empowers you to define and manage both cloud-based and on-premises resources using simple, human-readable configuration files. These files are not only easy to understand but also designed for versioning, reuse, and sharing, fostering collaboration and efficient infrastructure management.

Before delving into Terraform's capabilities, the first step is to install it on your system. Terraform is available for various operating systems and can be downloaded from the official website. For this book, we'll be using version 1.9.

macOS

Terraform can be installed easily on your Mac using a tool called homebrew, which helps you download and manage various software packages. If you don't already have homebrew installed, you can find instructions at https://docs.brew.sh/Installation.

Once you have homebrew, installing Terraform is a breeze. Just open your terminal and type the following commands:

```
brew tap hashicorp/tap
brew install hashicorp/tap/terraform
```

That's it! Terraform will be downloaded and installed on your Mac.

Windows

If your system is Windows, you can use Binary Download to install Terraform manually.

- **386**

  https://releases.hashicorp.com/terraform/1.8.2/
  terraform_1.8.2_windows_386.zip

- **AMD64**

  https://releases.hashicorp.com/terraform/1.8.2/
  terraform_1.8.2_windows_amd64.zip

Linux

If you're using a Linux system, you have several options for installing Terraform, depending on your distribution and preferred method. Here's a quick guide to get you up and running

Option 1: Installing with Homebrew

Homebrew is a popular package manager that simplifies the installation of software on Linux.

```
brew tap hashicorp/tap
brew install hashicorp/tap/terraform
```

Option 2: Installing on Ubuntu/Debian

For Ubuntu and Debian users, you can install Terraform directly using the official HashiCorp repository.

```
wget -O- https://apt.releases.hashicorp.com/gpg | sudo gpg
--dearmor -o /usr/share/keyrings/hashicorp-archive-keyring.gpg
echo "deb [signed-by=/usr/share/keyrings/hashicorp-archive-
keyring.gpg] https://apt.releases.hashicorp.com $(lsb_release
-cs) main" | sudo tee /etc/apt/sources.list.d/hashicorp.list
sudo apt update && sudo apt install terraform
```

Option 3: Installing on CentOS/RHEL

CentOS and RHEL users can install Terraform using the official HashiCorp
repository.

```
sudo yum install -y yum-utils
sudo yum-config-manager --add-repo https://rpm.releases.
hashicorp.com/RHEL/hashicorp.repo
sudo yum -y install terraform
```

Option 4: Installing on Amazon Linux

You can also install it on Amazon Linux.

```
sudo yum install -y yum-utils shadow-utils
sudo yum-config-manager --add-repo https://rpm.releases.
hashicorp.com/AmazonLinux/hashicorp.repo
sudo yum -y install terraform
```

Docker

If you prefer not to install Terraform directly on your system or if you're
using Docker, you can run Terraform in a container.

```
docker pull hashicorp/terraform
```

The Terraform team publishes a Docker image to this repository for each official release of Terraform CLI. Each versioned image includes the Terraform CLI release with the same version number. For example, the following command uses the latest tag to generate a plan using the most recent version of Terraform:

```
docker run -i -t hashicorp/terraform:latest plan
```

For production use, it's better to specify a specific version rather than using latest to ensure consistency across environments.

With these installation methods, you'll be ready to start using Terraform on your system in no time. Choose the method that best fits your setup, and let's move on to exploring Terraform's configuration language and basic commands.

Configuration Language

Terraform relies on the HashiCorp Configuration Language, a declarative language tailored for defining infrastructure configurations. Designed to be both human-readable and machine-friendly, HCL simplifies the process of describing your infrastructure's desired state, making it far easier than using generic formats.

So, why not just use JSON or YAML? While those formats are great for data serialization, they're not optimized for creating structured configurations. HCL strikes the perfect balance between simplicity and functionality. It offers a clean, easy-to-read syntax while enabling more advanced configurations through its declarative logic.

HCL's structure is built around key-value pairs and hierarchical blocks, which makes defining resources straightforward. This design doesn't just make life easier for developers—it also allows Terraform and other HashiCorp tools to provide clear error messages and an intuitive configuration experience.

The benefits of learning HCL go beyond just Terraform. It's the common language for all HashiCorp tools, including Vault and Nomad, meaning once you've mastered it, you'll find it easier to expand into other workflows and tools.

With HCL, you gain a robust and consistent way to manage and automate infrastructure. It's the backbone of efficient scaling and seamless integration across HashiCorp's ecosystem, empowering you to take your infrastructure automation to the next level.

Syntax and Structure of HCL

HCL is designed to be straightforward, with a clear and concise syntax that is easy to understand. A typical HCL script is composed of blocks, arguments, and expressions. Here's an overview of these components using a practical example of creating a cloud storage bucket on Google Cloud Platform (GCP):

```
terraform {
  required_providers {
    google = {
      source = "hashicorp/google"
      version = "5.38.0"
    }
  }
}

provider "google" {

  project = "terraform-made-easy"   #replace to your project id
  region  = "us-central1"
  zone    = "us-central1-a"
}
```

```
resource "google_storage_bucket" "default" {
 name            = "ivys_bucket_a"  # give your unique
                                      bucket name
 location      = "US"
 storage_class = "STANDARD"
}
```

Blocks

terraform {} is a block. In HCL, blocks are fundamental structural elements that define a set of related configuration settings. Each block starts with a type and is enclosed in curly braces: {}.

provider "google" {} is the second block. It is called a *provider block*, which defines the providers that interact with your infrastructure. Each provider block specifies the provider's settings.

Arguments and Expressions

Within the provider block, there are three *arguments* (project, region, and zone). We use them to specify the settings for resources. They are written as key-value pairs.

The third block is a *resource block*, which defines the specific infrastructure resource you want to create or manage (in this case, a storage bucket). In this example, we have three arguments (name, location, and storage_class). We use *expressions* to assign values to arguments. For example, location = "US" is an expression that sets the location of the bucket.

Variables

You can think of *variables* as placeholders that you can fill with specific values later. This makes your Terraform configurations more flexible and reusable. For example, you could define a variable for a region name and then set its value to us-central1 when you deploy your infrastructure in the region.

```
variable "region" {
  description = "The GCP region to deploy resources in"
  type        = string
  default     = "us-central1"
}
```

Instead of hard-coding values, you can simply reference variables within expressions, reducing redundancy and improving maintainability.

```
resource "google_compute_instance" "compute_instance" {
    name = var.instance_name
    machine_type = var.machine_type
    zone = var.zone
```

Outputs

Outputs are like the results of your Terraform configuration. They allow you to extract values from your infrastructure and use them for other purposes, such as in subsequent Terraform runs or in external scripts.

```
output "vpc_networks" {
  value = { for region, vpc in google_compute_network.vpc :
region => vpc.self_link }
}
```

Modules

Modules are reusable blocks of Terraform code that encapsulate a specific set of resources or functionality. You can think of them as prebuilt components that you can plug into your main configuration. Modules are reusable configurations that can be shared across different projects. They are defined in their own directory and can be referenced using the module block.

```
module "instance1"{
    source = "./modules/compute_instance"

    instance_name = "instance-1"
    machine_type = "e2-medium"
    zone = "us-central1-a"
    tags          = ["web", "dev"]
}
```

HCL's syntax offers a clear, organized approach to defining infrastructure as code. Its blocks, arguments, and expressions make it both accessible and powerful, providing a balance between simplicity and functionality. As you work more with HCL, you will find its structured nature and flexible components enhance your ability to manage complex infrastructure effectively.

Terraform Workflow

Now that you have a basic understanding of Terraform, it's time to dive into its workflow and essential commands. To truly grasp how Terraform works, it's best to get hands-on experience with its core commands.

Learning by doing is one of the most effective ways to master new skills. So, let's get started! Open up your terminal, set up a new directory for your Terraform project, and start practicing these commands. Don't worry if you make mistakes—each command is a step toward becoming proficient. Here's a quick overview to guide your practice:

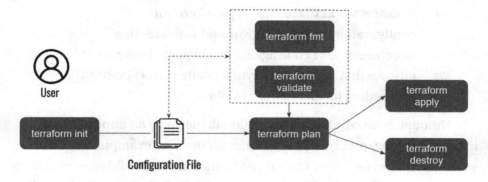

Figure 2-1. *Terraform Workflow: From Configuration to Execution*

> **init**: Initialize your workspace so Terraform can apply your code.
>
> **write**: Express your infrastructure needs using code. This is just like telling Terraform what you want in a language it understands.
>
> **plan**: Get a sneak peek at all the changes Terraform is about to make so you're always in the know and avoid the human-error.
>
> **apply**: Execute the changes from your plan, and watch Terraform create, update, or destroy resources as needed.

In the dotted box, you can see two commands: `terraform fmt` and `terraform validate`.

- **terraform fmt** formats your Terraform code to follow a consistent style, making it more readable and maintainable. While it's not mandatory, running **terraform fmt** ensures your code adheres to the standard conventions, reducing errors caused by inconsistent formatting.

- **terraform validate** checks your Terraform configuration for syntax errors and validates the structure of your code against the expected schema. It ensures that your code is syntactically correct before proceeding further in the workflow.

Although both commands are optional, they play an important role in improving the quality of your Terraform code. For example, `terraform validate` checks for errors in your configuration that would prevent it from being successfully applied. If issues are found, Terraform won't proceed to the planning or applying stages. Instead, it provides clear feedback, allowing you to fix the problems before moving forward.

These steps act as guardrails, helping you write cleaner, error-free code before moving forward to the next stages of planning and applying your infrastructure changes.

Initialize Terraform

Before you can start working with Terraform, you need to initialize your working directory. This step sets up the necessary environment and downloads the provider plugins required for your configuration. The first command is `terraform init`.

```
$ terraform init

Terraform initialized in an empty directory!

The directory has no Terraform configuration files. You may
begin working with Terraform immediately by creating Terraform
configuration files.
```

While the previous example demonstrated `terraform init` in an empty directory, its behavior might differ when used in a directory containing configuration files. For instance, if you have existing Terraform configuration files, `terraform init` will automatically detect and initialize them.

```
$ terraform init

Initializing the backend...

Initializing provider plugins...
- Reusing previous version of hashicorp/google from the
  dependency lock file
- Using previously-installed hashicorp/google v5.38.0

Terraform has been successfully initialized!
```

You may now begin working with Terraform. Try running "terraform plan" to see any changes that are required for your infrastructure. All Terraform commands should now work.

If you ever set or change modules or backend configuration for Terraform, rerun this command to reinitialize your working directory. If you forget, other commands will detect it and remind you to do so if necessary.

The terraform init command may seem simple, but it performs several key tasks to prepare your Terraform environment. Here's a breakdown of what happens:

1. **Initialize the Back End**

   Terraform uses a back end to manage how state is stored and how operations are performed. A back end is a component that determines where and how Terraform's state is saved. It could be local (storing the state file on your local machine) or remote (storing the state file in a shared location such as an /Google Cloud Storage, Azure Storage, or Terraform Cloud). When you run the command, it initializes the backend configuration you've specified, ensuring that Terraform can properly manage and access your state data.

2. **Download and Install Provider Plugins**

   Terraform relies on provider plugins to interact
   with various cloud platforms and services. It
   automatically downloads and installs these plugins
   based on the configurations in your Terraform files.
   In this case, it is `hashicorp/google v5.38.0`.

3. **Set Up Modules**

   If your configuration uses prebuilt modules
   (reusable blocks of code), the command ensures
   they are downloaded and set up correctly and
   all the building blocks your code depends on are
   ready to go.

4. **Configure Local State**

   Terraform maintains the state of your infrastructure
   in a file called `terraform.tfstate`. This state file
   keeps track of the resources Terraform manages,
   their configurations, and their current status. During
   initialization, `terraform init` sets up the local state
   file if it's not already present. This step is crucial for
   Terraform to accurately manage and track changes
   to your infrastructure.

Write Configuration Files

This step isn't for Terraform—it's for you! Here, you define the desired state
of your infrastructure in configuration files, which act as the blueprint for
what Terraform will build. These files typically use the `.tf` extension and
contain the instructions Terraform needs to understand and provision
your infrastructure.

For example, a commonly used file might be called main.tf. The following is a sample snippet to give you an idea of how a configuration file looks:

```
# the configuration file - main.tf

terraform {
  required_providers {
    google = {
      source = "hashicorp/google"
      version = "5.38.0"
    }
  }
}

provider "google" {

  project = "terraform-made-easy"  #replace to your project id
  region  = "us-central1"
  zone    = "us-central1-a"
}

resource "google_storage_bucket" "default" {
 name             = "ivys_bucket_a"  # give your unique
                    bucket name
 location         = "US"
 storage_class = "STANDARD"
}
```

Plan the Changes

Before applying any changes, it's a good practice to preview what Terraform will do. The command terraform plan is the key for understanding the changes that will be applied to your infrastructure

33

before actually making those changes. After executing the command, it will examine your current state and compare it to the desired state defined in your Terraform configurations (e.g., main.tf)

For each resource that is part of the plan, Terraform indicates the action it will take. Common actions include the following:

- + for resources that will be added

- - for resources that will be destroyed

- ~ for resources that will be modified

If Terraform determines that no changes are necessary for resource instances or root module output values, terraform plan will report that no actions need to be taken. This proactive approach ensures a thorough understanding of configuration drift and promotes a secure environment for implementing changes.

```
$ terraform plan
```

Terraform used the selected providers to generate the following execution plan. Resource actions are indicated with the following symbols:
  + create

Terraform will perform the following actions:

```
  # google_storage_bucket.default will be created
  + resource "google_storage_bucket" "default" {
      + effective_labels            = (known after apply)
      + force_destroy               = false
      + id                          = (known after apply)
      + location                    = "US"
      + name                        = "ivys_bucket_a"
      + project                     = (known after apply)
      + project_number              = (known after apply)
```

```
    + public_access_prevention    = (known after apply)
    + rpo                         = (known after apply)
    + self_link                   = (known after apply)
    + storage_class               = "STANDARD"
    + terraform_labels            = (known after apply)
    + uniform_bucket_level_access = (known after apply)
    + url                         = (known after apply)
  }
Plan: 1 to add, 0 to change, 0 to destroy.
```

Apply the Changes

terraform apply is used to apply the changes specified in the plan. Upon executing the command, it carefully reviews the proposed changes and prompts you to confirm that you want to apply the changes. You need to type yes to proceed or use the --auto-approve flag. Then Terraform will begin the execution process, applying the changes outlined in the execution plan.

The output will display real-time feedback on each step of the application process. You'll see information about the resources being created, modified, or destroyed. If there are errors or issues, Terraform will provide relevant information to help you understand what went wrong. Once the apply process is complete, Terraform will provide a summary of the changes applied, any errors encountered, and the time taken to complete the operation.

```
$ terraform apply --auto-approve
```

Terraform used the selected providers to generate the following execution plan. Resource actions are indicated with the following symbols:

```
  + create
Terraform will perform the following actions:
```

```
    # google_storage_bucket.default will be created
    + resource "google_storage_bucket" "default" {
        + effective_labels            = (known after apply)
        + force_destroy               = false
        + id                          = (known after apply)
        + location                    = "US"
        + name                        = "ivys_bucket_a"
        + project                     = (known after apply)
        + project_number              = (known after apply)
        + public_access_prevention    = (known after apply)
        + rpo                         = (known after apply)
        + self_link                   = (known after apply)
        + storage_class               = "STANDARD"
        + terraform_labels            = (known after apply)
        + uniform_bucket_level_access = (known after apply)
        + url                         = (known after apply)
    }

Plan: 1 to add, 0 to change, 0 to destroy.
google_storage_bucket.default: Creating...
google_storage_bucket.default: Creation complete after 2s
[id=ivys_bucket_a]

Apply complete! Resources: 1 added, 0 changed, 0 destroyed.
```

Manage or Destroy Resources

If you need to remove all the resources managed by Terraform, you can use
the terraform destroy command. This command will delete all resources
defined in your configuration. Similar to terraform apply, it prompts
for confirmation before proceeding, unless you use the --auto-approve
flag. However, using --auto-approve is generally discouraged to avoid
unintentional deletions.

The following is an example of deleting a storage bucket resource using the terraform destroy command:

```
$ terraform destroy
google_storage_bucket.default: Refreshing state... [id=ivys_
bucket_a]
```

Terraform used the selected providers to generate the following execution plan. Resource actions are indicated with the following symbols:
  - destroy

Terraform will perform the following actions:

```
  # google_storage_bucket.default will be destroyed
  - resource "google_storage_bucket" "default" {
      - default_event_based_hold    = false -> null
      - effective_labels            = {} -> null
      - enable_object_retention     = false -> null
      - force_destroy               = false -> null
      - id                          = "ivys_bucket_a" -> null
      - labels                      = {} -> null
      - location                    = "US" -> null
      - name                        = "ivys_bucket_a" -> null
      - project                     = "terraform-made-
                                      easy" -> null
      - project_number              = 510440994482 -> null
      - public_access_prevention    = "inherited" -> null
      - requester_pays              = false -> null
      - rpo                         = "DEFAULT" -> null
      - self_link                   = "https://www.googleapis.
                                      com/storage/v1/b/ivys_
                                      bucket_a" -> null
      - storage_class               = "STANDARD" -> null
```

```
  - terraform_labels            = {} -> null
  - uniform_bucket_level_access = false -> null
  - url                         = "gs://ivys_
                                    bucket_a" -> null

  - soft_delete_policy {
    - effective_time            = "2024-08-31T16:00:
                                    00.218Z" -> null
    - retention_duration_seconds = 604800 -> null
    }
  }
```

Plan: 0 to add, 0 to change, 1 to destroy.

Do you really want to destroy all resources?
  Terraform will destroy all your managed infrastructure, as
  shown above.
  There is no undo. Only 'yes' will be accepted to confirm.

  Enter a value: yes

```
google_storage_bucket.default: Destroying... [id=ivys_bucket_a]
google_storage_bucket.default: Destruction complete after 1s
```

Destroy complete! Resources: 1 destroyed.

While terraform destroy is a powerful tool for managing and cleaning up your infrastructure, it demands careful handling.

Before executing it, always review the execution plan in detail to ensure you understand exactly which resources will be deleted. Additionally, consult with your team or key stakeholders to confirm that the planned deletions align with operational needs and won't disrupt ongoing services. Clear communication and verification can prevent accidental data loss or outages.

Summary

In this chapter, you embarked on a journey into the world of Terraform, covering several essential topics to get you started. Here's a quick recap of what we covered:

- **Installing Terraform**: You learned how to set up Terraform on your machine, ensuring you're ready to manage infrastructure as code.

- **Understanding HCL**: You explored HCL, diving into its syntax and structure. You saw how HCL uses blocks, arguments, and expressions to define your infrastructure.

- **Terraform Workflow**: You became familiar with the core commands that drive Terraform's workflow:

    - `terraform init`: Sets up your environment by initializing the back end and downloading necessary plugins.

    - `terraform fmt`: Formats your Terraform code to follow a consistent style, making it more readable and maintainable.

    - `terraform validate`: Checks your Terraform configuration for syntax errors and validates the structure of your code against the expected schema.

    - `terraform plan`: Prepares a detailed plan of the changes Terraform will make to your infrastructure.

- `terraform apply`: Executes the plan and applies the changes to create or update resources.

- `terraform destroy`: Deletes all resources specified in your configuration, useful for cleanup but requiring careful use.

With these basics in place, you're well-equipped to start managing infrastructure with Terraform. In the next chapter, we'll dive deeper into more advanced commands and functionalities, expanding your toolkit and helping you harness the full power of Terraform. Keep experimenting and practicing—there's always much more to explore!

## CHAPTER 3

Key Concepts of Terraform

In the previous chapter, we laid a strong foundation for your Terraform journey by exploring its core workflow and essential commands. Now, it's time to take your skills to the next level and tackle the complexities of real-world infrastructure management.

Imagine managing a large-scale project that spans multiple environments and involves hundreds of variables, intricate dependencies, and a team of collaborators. How do you ensure consistency, efficiency, and scalability in such a dynamic environment?

In this chapter, we'll equip you with advanced techniques to tackle these challenges head on. You'll learn how to master versatile providers, effectively manage variables, create and reuse modules, handle complex dependencies, and maintain state consistency in collaborative projects. By the end of the chapter, you'll have the skills to confidently manage large-scale infrastructure with Terraform, ensuring your deployments are robust, maintainable, and scalable.

Get ready to elevate your Terraform skills to new heights!

© Ivy Wang 2024
I. Wang, *Terraform Made Easy*, https://doi.org/10.1007/979-8-8688-1010-7_3

Providers for Everybody

A Terraform provider acts as a bridge between Terraform and external application programming interfaces (APIs), allowing Terraform to interface with cloud providers, software-as-a-service (SaaS) platforms, and other services. Providers are crucial to Terraform's ability to manage and interact with a wide range of resources, making them integral to its overall functionality.

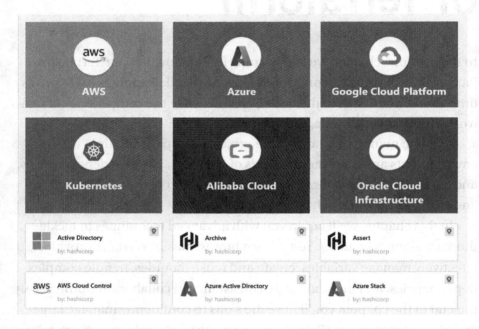

Figure 3-1. *Examples of Providers on the Terraform Website*

Versatility and Widespread Adoption

One of Terraform's strengths is its extensive array of providers, which contribute to its versatility and broad adoption. Each provider introduces a unique set of resource types and data sources that Terraform can manage. This modular design allows each provider to be distributed separately from Terraform, following its own release schedule and versioning system. Providers also come with their own documentation, which details the available resources, data sources, and configurable options.

Terraform Registry

The Terraform Registry serves as the primary directory for publicly available Terraform providers. It hosts a vast selection of providers for major infrastructure platforms and includes comprehensive documentation for each. These providers are developed by HashiCorp, third-party vendors, and the Terraform community. As of now, the Registry features more than 4,000 providers, along with an extensive library of more than 17,000 modules, policies, and runnable tasks.

Types of Providers

Providers in the Terraform Registry are categorized based on who maintains them, which is indicated by specific badges:

- **Official Providers**: Developed and maintained by HashiCorp, these providers are labeled as "official" and are generally the most reliable, receiving regular updates and support.

- **Partner Providers**: These are maintained by third-party technology vendors who are part of the HashiCorp Technology Partner Program. They are marked as "partner" providers and typically offer robust support and updates.

- **Community Providers**: Developed and maintained by individual community members or groups, these providers often address niche or emerging services. They are marked as "community" and can vary in terms of support and update frequency.

- **Archived Providers**: These providers are no longer actively maintained or supported. Marked as "archived," they should be used with caution, as they may not receive updates or bug fixes.

Independent Releases and Maintenance

The independence of each provider ensures that they can rapidly adapt to changes in their respective services and APIs. This flexibility allows providers to keep pace with the evolving landscape of infrastructure and services, ensuring that Terraform remains a powerful and up-to-date tool for managing your infrastructure.

This modular and adaptable approach is what makes Terraform a versatile and widely adopted solution for infrastructure as code. By understanding and leveraging providers effectively, you can leverage the full potential of Terraform in managing your infrastructure.

Installing and Managing Provider Versions

Terraform handles provider installation and version management during the `terraform init` phase of your workflow. Providers can be sourced from the public registry, a local registry, or a mirror. If a provider with the required version is already present in the `.terraform` subdirectory, Terraform will use it without re-downloading. However, specifying a different version in your configuration file will trigger Terraform to fetch the new version. It's important to reinitialize your working directory (`terraform init`) whenever you update your configuration's providers to ensure everything is up-to-date.

Optimizing Provider Management

To enhance efficiency, particularly in environments with limited bandwidth or where time is critical, Terraform supports an optional plugin cache. You can configure this cache using the `plugin_cache_dir` setting in your CLI configuration file (`terraform.rc` or `.terraformrc`). This cache stores previously downloaded providers, reducing the need for repeated downloads and speeding up the initialization process.

```
plugin_cache_dir = "$HOME/.terraform.d/plugin-cache"
```

Examples of Providers

Understanding Provider Requirements

In Terraform, each module must specify the providers it requires to manage the infrastructure. Providers are essential because they allow Terraform to interact with various cloud platforms and services. These requirements are declared within a `required_providers` block, which is nested inside the top-level `terraform` block.

Here's a Google provider example:

```
terraform {
  required_providers {
    google = {
      source = "hashicorp/google"
      version = "5.38.0"
    }
  }
}
```

A provider requirement consists of the following:

- **Local Name**: The provider's unique identifier within the module

- **Source Location**: The global source address where Terraform can find the provider (e.g., `hashicorp/google`)

- **Version Constraint**: Specifies the versions of the provider that the module is compatible with (e.g., `version = "5.38.0"`)

AWS Provider Example

The AWS provider allows Terraform to manage AWS resources like EC2 instances, S3 buckets, and RDS databases.

```
provider "aws" {
  region = "us-west-2"
}
resource "aws_instance" "example" {
  ami          = "ami-0c55b159cbfafe1f0"
  instance_type = "t2.micro"
}
```

The `provider` {} block configures the AWS provider, specifying the us-west-2 region. All AWS resources managed by Terraform in this module will be created in this region.

The `resource` {} block defines an EC2 instance. The `ami` specifies the Amazon Machine Image (AMI) ID to be used, while the `instance_type` defines the type of EC2 instance (`t2.micro`), which is suitable for lightweight applications or development environments.

Azure Provider Example

The Azure provider lets Terraform manage Azure resources such as virtual machines, storage accounts, and SQL databases.

```
provider "azurerm" {
  features {}
}

resource "azurerm_resource_group" "example" {
  name     = "example-resources"
  location = "West US"
}

resource "azurerm_virtual_network" "example" {
  name                = "example-network"
  address_space       = ["10.0.0.0/16"]
  location            = azurerm_resource_group.example.location
  resource_group_name = azurerm_resource_group.example.name
}
```

The provider {} block configures the Azure Resource Manager provider. The features {} block is necessary even if no specific settings are applied, enabling the default features for the provider.

The azurerm_resource_group {} block creates a resource group named example-resources in the West US region.

The resource {} block defines a virtual network (VNet) named example-network within the example-resources resource group. The address_space defines the IP address range for the VNet, and the location and resource_group_name reference the previously created resource group.

GitHub Provider Example

The GitHub provider in Terraform allows you to manage GitHub resources like repositories, teams, and memberships programmatically. This enables you to automate your GitHub workflows and maintain consistency across your projects.

```
provider "github" {
  token = var.github_token
}

resource "github_repository" "example" {
  name        = "example-repo"
  description = "My awesome repository"
  private     = false
}
```

In this example, the GitHub provider is configured using a personal access token stored in the `github_token` variable. The `github_repository` resource creates a new repository named `example-repo`, with a description and public visibility. This setup is useful for automating the creation and management of GitHub repositories directly from your Terraform code.

Kubernetes Provider Example

The Kubernetes provider allows Terraform to manage Kubernetes resources, making it easier to deploy and scale applications within your Kubernetes cluster.

```
provider "kubernetes" {
  config_path = "~/.kube/config"
}

resource "kubernetes_namespace" "example" {
  metadata {
    name = "example-namespace"
```

```
    }
}
resource "kubernetes_deployment" "example" {
  metadata {
    name      = "nginx-deployment"
    namespace = kubernetes_namespace.example.metadata[0].name
  }
  spec {
    replicas = 2
    selector {
      match_labels = {
        App = "nginx"
      }
    }
    template {
      metadata {
        labels = {
          App = "nginx"
        }
      }
      spec {
        container {
          name  = "nginx"
          image = "nginx:1.14.2"
          ports {
            container_port = 80
          }
        }
      }
    }
  }
}
```

In this example, the Kubernetes provider connects to your cluster using the configuration file specified in `config_path`. A new namespace called `example-namespace` is created using the `kubernetes_namespace` resource. The `kubernetes_deployment` resource defines a deployment of two NGINX pods within this namespace. The deployment ensures that the NGINX service is consistently running and accessible on port 80.

MongoDB Atlas Provider Example

The MongoDB Atlas provider lets you manage MongoDB Atlas resources, such as clusters, databases, and users, through Terraform. This helps in automating database infrastructure in a cloud environment.

```
provider "mongodbatlas" {
  public_key  = var.mongodb_public_key
  private_key = var.mongodb_private_key
}

resource "mongodbatlas_cluster" "example" {
  project_id   = var.project_id
  name         = "example-cluster"
  cluster_type = "REPLICASET"
  provider_name = "AWS"
  provider_instance_size_name = "M10"
  provider_region_name = "US_EAST_1"
}
```

In this example, the MongoDB Atlas provider is configured using the public and private keys stored in variables. The `mongodbatlas_cluster` resource creates a MongoDB cluster named `example-cluster` within a specified project. The cluster is set up as a replica set on AWS, with an instance size of M10 in the US_EAST_1 region. This configuration is ideal for managing and scaling your MongoDB clusters automatically.

All these examples demonstrate how Terraform can be used to manage diverse infrastructure resources, from code repositories and Kubernetes clusters to cloud-based databases, all from a unified framework. By leveraging these providers, you can automate complex infrastructure tasks, ensuring consistency and reliability across your environments.

Variables and Outputs

I understand that working with providers can sometimes feel overwhelming—don't worry, you're not alone in this! It's perfectly normal to feel that way at first. Just like any new skill, the more you practice and learn, the more confident you'll become in managing them effectively.

Now, we're shifting our focus to a critical aspect of Terraform: **variables and outputs**. Think of them as the heartbeat of Terraform— essential for powering its efficiency and simplicity. This section introduces new terms and concepts, but don't let that intimidate you. Take your time, move at your own pace, and remember, it's okay to slow down and fully absorb the information.

You'll soon find that it's not as complex as it seems. Let's dive into it step-by-step. As you've seen in the previous chapters, Terraform, as a declarative language, uses various block types—each with its distinct role in managing infrastructure resources. These block types include **input variables**, **output variables**, and **local values**.

Input Variables

Input variables act as parameters for a Terraform module, allowing users to customize its behavior without modifying the source code. They function similarly to function arguments, enhancing flexibility and reusability. By defining input variables, module creators empower users to adjust settings according to their specific needs, which promotes organization and simplifies module sharing.

For instance, consider a Terraform module that provisions cloud resources. Input variables enable you to customize aspects such as instance size, region, or disk type, without delving into the module's inner workings. This customization streamlines collaboration and maintains consistency across infrastructure setups.

Defining Input Variables

Here's how to define input variables in Terraform:

```
# Define Input Variables

variable "machine_type" {
  description = "The machine type for the Compute Engine
  instance"
  default     = "n1-standard-1"
}
variable "zone" {
  description = "The zone for the Compute Engine instance"
  default     = "us-central1-a"
}
```

In this example, machine_type and zone are the names of the variables. These names must be unique within the module and are used to assign and reference values.

Note that certain names are reserved for meta-arguments and cannot be used as variable names. These include source, version, providers, count, for_each, lifecycle, depends_on, and locals.

Understanding Variable Arguments

When working with Terraform, variables are a powerful tool that allow you to customize and manage your infrastructure configurations efficiently. In Terraform, a variable block can be fine-tuned with several optional arguments that add flexibility, control, and clarity to your code. Let's explore each of these arguments in detail.

```
variable "project_id" {
  description = "The ID of the GCP project"
  type        = string
  default     = "terraform-made-easy"
}
```

In the example, there are three variable arguments: `description`, `default`, and `type`.

- **description**: The argument is used to provide a human-readable explanation of what the variable is for. This is particularly useful for making your Terraform code more understandable.

- **default**: This argument allows you to set a default value for a variable. This means that if the user does not provide a value, Terraform will automatically use the default. In this case, the default `project_id` is `terraform-made-easy.` This approach simplifies your configuration by reducing the number of required inputs.

- **type**: This argument within a variable block defines what kind of values are allowed for that variable. By setting a type constraint, you ensure that users provide values that are appropriate for the variable, which helps prevent errors and improves the clarity of your configuration.

When you specify the type argument, Terraform enforces that only values of the defined type can be assigned to the variable. This reduces the risk of mistakes and makes your Terraform code more robust. If you omit the type argument, Terraform will accept any value, which can lead to unpredictable behavior.

Here are some of the types you can specify:

- **Primitive Types**: string, number, and bool

- **Complex Types**: list, set, map, object, and tuple

If you use the any keyword, the variable can accept values of any type. This is useful when you want to allow flexibility in what can be provided. For example:

```
variable "dynamic_value" {
  description = "A value of any type"
  type        = any
}
```

validation: This argument allows you to enforce rules on variable values beyond just type constraints. This is useful for ensuring that user inputs meet specific criteria, such as a string following a certain pattern or a number within a range.

```
variable "machine_type" {
  description = "The type of GCP machine to use for the
  instances"
  type        = string
  default     = "e2-medium"

  validation {
    condition       = contains(["e2-micro", "e2-small", "e2-
                      medium"], var.machine_type)
```

```
    error_message = "The machine type must be one of 'e2-
    micro', 'e2-small', or 'e2-medium'."
  }
}

resource "google_compute_instance" "validated" {
  name         = "vm-instance"
  machine_type = var.machine_type
  project      = var.project_id
  zone         = "us-central1-a"

  boot_disk {
    initialize_params {
      image = "debian-cloud/debian-10"
    }
  }
}
```

In this example, the validation {} block ensures that the machine_ type is one of the allowed values. If a user attempts to use a different machine type, Terraform will return an error with the specified error_ message.

nullable: This argument controls whether a variable can be assigned a null value. By default, variables in Terraform can accept null unless specified otherwise. This flexibility allows users to either provide a specific value or leave the variable as null, which can be useful in various scenarios.

sensitive: This argument is used to mask sensitive information, such as passwords or API keys, in Terraform's output and logs. By marking a variable as sensitive, you ensure that its value is hidden, adding an extra layer of security and preventing accidental exposure.

```
variable "user_name" {
  type    = string
```

```
nullable = false
sensitive = true
}
```

The previous is an example using both `nullable` and `sensitive` arguments together to control the nullability and visibility of a variable. By setting nullable argument to `false`, it ensures the `user_name` value must be provided. By setting sensitive arguments to `true`, Terraform will not show its value in the console output, ensuring that sensitive user information remains confidential.

Environment Variables

Environment variables in Terraform provide a flexible way to configure Terraform's behavior without embedding sensitive or environment-specific values directly in your configuration files. This approach enhances security and adaptability by allowing you to manage sensitive information, such as credentials, more securely.

Setting Environment Variables

You can set environment variables in your shell to customize Terraform's behavior. Terraform recognizes environment variables prefixed with TF_VAR_ followed by the variable name. For example, if you have a variable named `region` in your Terraform configuration, you can set its value using the environment variable TF_VAR_region.

```
#windows
export TF_VAR_region="eu-west-3"

#macOS /Linux
export TF_VAR_region="eu-west-3"
```

Using Environment Variables

Step 1: Define variable in the configuration file (`variables.tf`).

```
variable "region" {
  description = "GCP project region"
  type        = string
}
```

Step 2: Set the environment variable in the shell.

```
export TF_VAR_region="eu-west-3"
```

Step 3: Apply the Terraform configuration.

```
terraform apply
```

Undeclared Variables

Undeclared variables in Terraform refer to variables that are used in the configuration but have not been explicitly declared using a `variable` block. These variables can still be set through environment variables, in `.tfvars` files, or directly at the command line when executing Terraform commands.

Behavior of Undeclared Variables:

- **Environment Variables**: Terraform does not issue a warning or error if you set an environment variable for an undeclared variable. This is because Terraform accepts these values without validating if the corresponding variable is declared in the configuration.

- **.tfvars Files**: If you provide values for undeclared variables in a `.tfvars` file, Terraform will issue a warning. This helps you catch cases where a variable might be missing from your configuration, potentially due to a typo or oversight.

Correct variable declaration:

```
variable "product" {
  type = string
}
```

Incorrect .tfvars file:

```
product  = "Product"
```

Terraform will warn that there is no declared variable named product, helping you spot the mistake. If you use .tfvars files across multiple configurations and expect these warnings, you can use the -compact-warnings option to simplify your output.

If you provide values for undeclared variables on the command line, Terraform will return an error. To avoid this, either declare the variable in your configuration file or remove the value from your command.

While undeclared variables offer flexibility, it's generally a good practice to declare variables in your configuration files. This makes the configuration more readable and maintainable. For sensitive information like API keys or passwords, use environment variables to avoid hardcoding these values in your configuration files.

Output Variables

Output variables in Terraform are essential for sharing information about your infrastructure after running terraform apply. They allow you to expose key details such as IP addresses, DNS names, or other attributes of your infrastructure components. This information can be crucial for integrating with other configurations, scripts, or team members.

Output variables are similar to return values in other programming languages and serve several key purposes:

- **Exposing Information to Parent Modules**: Child modules can reveal specific resource attributes to their parent modules using outputs.

- **Command-Line Display**: The root module can display values in the CLI after running `terraform apply`.

- **Remote State Access**: When using remote state, outputs from the root module can be accessed by other configurations through the `terraform_remote_state` data source.

Terraform-managed resource instances export attributes that can be used elsewhere, and outputs help expose this information to users.

Declaring Output Values

To declare an output value, use the `output` block in your Terraform configuration. This block specifies the information to be exposed and how it should be formatted.

```
output "vpc_network_name" {
  value = google_compute_network.vpc_network.name
}
```

In this example, `vpc_network_name` is the name of the output, and it returns the name of the `google_compute_network` resource.

Accessing Outputs from Child Modules

In a typical Terraform setup, you may have a root module, parent modules, and child modules. To access an output from a child module, use the syntax `module.<MODULE_NAME>.<OUTPUT_NAME>`.

In this example, vpc is the name of the module, and the subnet_name is an output variable defined within the vpc module.

```
output "subnet_name" {
  value = module.vpc.subnet_name
}
```

Optional Arguments for Output Blocks

The output block in Terraform provides several optional arguments to enhance the clarity and precision of your configurations. These options allow you to define custom conditions, specify sensitivity, and declare dependencies.

Here is an example that includes all optional arguments in an output block:

```
output "subnet_name" {
  value       = module.vpc.subnet_name
  description = "The name of the subnet created in the VPC"
  sensitive   = true
  condition   = length(module.vpc.subnet_name) > 4
  depends_on  = [module.vpc]
}
```

- **value**: Specifies the value to be output, which is the subnet name from the vpc module.

- **condition**: Outputs the value only if the condition is true; in this case, the condition ensures that the output is provided only if the subnet name is longer than four characters.

- **depends_on**: Explicitly declares that this output depends on the vpc module, ensuring proper ordering of resource creation.

By effectively using output variables and their optional arguments, you can create more dynamic, secure, and maintainable Terraform configurations. This approach enhances the integration of your infrastructure code and provides clear, actionable information throughout your infrastructure lifecycle.

Local Values

Local values in Terraform allow you to assign a name to an expression, making it easier to reuse that expression throughout a module. Think of local values as temporary variables within a function that can help simplify and streamline your configuration.

Local values can be particularly useful when a specific value or calculation is used multiple times in your Terraform configuration. Instead of repeating the same expression, you can define it once as a local value and refer to it by name. This approach makes your configuration more manageable and less prone to errors. However, it's important to use local values judiciously. Overusing them can obscure the actual values and make your configuration harder to read and maintain.

Best Practices:

- **Use Moderately**: Define local values for expressions or values that are used frequently or are likely to change. Avoid overcomplicating your configuration with too many local values.

- **Centralized Updates**: When a local value changes, you need to update it in only one place. This centralization simplifies maintenance and reduces the risk of inconsistencies.

Declaring Local Values

You can use the `locals {}` block to declare a local value. Here's an example that defines `project_id` and `region` as local values:

```
locals {
  project_id = "project id"
  region     = "us-central1"
}
```

Using Local Values

Once declared, local values can be referenced in your Terraform configuration using the syntax `local.<NAME>`. This makes it easy to incorporate the local values throughout your resources. Here's how you might use these local values:

```
resource "google_storage_bucket" "bucket1" {
  name          = "example-bucket1"
  location      = "EU"
  project       = local.project_id
  force_destroy = true
}

resource "google_storage_bucket" "bucket2" {
  name          = "example-bucket2"
  location      = "EU"
  project       = local.project_id
  force_destroy = true
}
```

In this example, using local values simplifies maintenance, reduces errors, and improves readability. By defining the `project_id` and `region` in the locals block, you need to update these values in only one place, rather than in each resource block. This approach minimizes the risk of inconsistencies or typos, as the values are defined once and reused throughout the configuration.

Leveraging the .tfvars Files

When managing infrastructure, it's common to configure various input variables for different aspects of your setup, such as instance types, region settings, and service account configurations. While you can hard-code these values directly into your Terraform configuration files, using a .tfvars file offers a more flexible and organized approach.

What Are .tfvars Files?

The .tfvars files are used to specify values for variables defined in your Terraform configuration. By separating variable definitions from their values, you can easily switch between different configurations or environments without altering the core logic of your Terraform scripts. This separation allows for a cleaner and more maintainable infrastructure codebase.

How to Use .tfvars Files?

Step 1. Define variables in a .tf file.

```
# variables.tf
variable "project" {
  description = " project ID"
  type        = string
}

variable "region" {
  description = "The GCP region"
  type        = string
}
```

```
variable "machine_type" {
  description = "The GCP machine type"
  type        = string
  default     = "n1-standard-1"
}
```

Step 2. Create a .tfvars file.

```
# tf.tfvars
project      = "project-id"
region       = "us-west1"
machine_type = "n1-standard-2"
```

Step 3: Reference these variables in your Terraform configuration file.

```
# main.tf

provider "google" {
  project = var.project
  region  = var.region
}

resource "google_compute_instance" "default" {
  name         = "terraform-instance"
  machine_type = var.machine_type
  zone         = "${var.region}-3"

  boot_disk {
    initialize_params {
      image = "debian-cloud/debian-10"
    }
  }

  network_interface {
    network = "default"
```

```
  access_config {
  }
 }
}
```

When you run Terraform `apply` commands, it will automatically read and use the values from the `tf.tfvars` file and then apply them in the configuration.

Managing Multiple Environments

A common practice is to manage configurations for different environments, such as development, staging, and production. To facilitate this, you can create separate `.tfvars` files for each environment. This allows you to maintain environment-specific settings without modifying the main Terraform configuration files.

Each of these `.tfvars` files will contain the variable values specific to that environment.

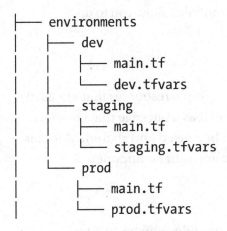

```
├── environments
│   ├── dev
│   │   ├── main.tf
│   │   └── dev.tfvars
│   ├── staging
│   │   ├── main.tf
│   │   └── staging.tfvars
│   └── prod
│       ├── main.tf
│       └── prod.tfvars
```

To apply the configuration for a specific environment, we can use the `-var-file` option when running Terraform commands. For example, to apply the development environment configuration, we would run this:

```
terraform apply -var-file="dev.tfvars"
```

Similarly, to apply the staging or production environment configurations, we can run this:

```
terraform apply -var-file="staging.tfvars"
terraform apply -var-file="prod.tfvars"
```

By using multiple .tfvars files, we can ensure that each environment is configured correctly without manual changes to the configuration files. This method enhances the flexibility and maintainability of your infrastructure code, allowing for seamless transitions between environments and reducing the risk of configuration errors.

Understand Modules

Up until now, you've likely been working with variables in Terraform—those handy inputs that let you customize your infrastructure without hard-coding values. But what if you could take that customization a step further? What if you could package entire sets of resources, complete with their own variables, into a reusable unit? That's precisely what modules allow you to do.

What Is a Module?

A module in Terraform is a container for multiple resources that are used together to achieve a specific goal. Think of it as a package that contains a set of Terraform configurations that can be reused and shared. Modules can include variables, outputs, resources, and other components.

Root Module

Every Terraform configuration has a root module, which is the top-level module in your configuration. It consists of the resources and configurations defined in the .tf files in your main working directory. When you run terraform init, terraform plan, or terraform apply in a directory, Terraform will treat that directory as the root module.

Child Module

A module that is called by another module (usually the root module) is referred to as a *child module*. Child modules can be reused multiple times in different configurations or even within the same configuration.

Here is a module that manages a GCP storage bucket:

```
modules/
    └── gcs_bucket/
         ├── main.tf
         ├── variables.tf
         └── outputs.tf
```

This module can then be called from the main Terraform configuration file, allowing you to create the bucket with specific attributes.

```
provider "google" {
  project = "project  id"
  region  = "us-west1"
}

module "gcs_bucket" {
  source      = "./modules/gcs_bucket"
  bucket_name = "unique-bucket-name"
  location    = "US"
  environment = "production"
}

output "gcs_bucket_url" {
  value = module.gcs_bucket.bucket_url
}
```

Local Module

This is a local module stored locally in your project directory. It's not published to any registry. When referenced, it uses a path relative to the current working directory. For example, `source = "./modules/gcs_bucket"`.

Published Module

A published module that has been uploaded to a Terraform Registry or hosted on a Version Control System (VCS) like GitHub. These modules can be shared and reused across different projects. For example, `source = "terraform-google-modules/cloud-storage/google"`.

The `Terraform Registry` hosts a broad collection of publicly available Terraform modules for configuring many kinds of common infrastructure. These modules are free to use, and Terraform can download them automatically if you specify the appropriate source and version in a module call block.

Module Block

A module block in Terraform is how you incorporate and utilize a module within your infrastructure code. Modules enable you to organize your Terraform configurations into smaller, reusable components, making it easier to manage infrastructure as code, particularly in complex environments.

```
provider "google" {
  project = "project  id"
  region  = "us-west1"
}
```

```
module "gcs_bucket" {
  source      = "./modules/gcs_bucket"
  bucket_name = "unique-bucket-name"
  location    = "US"
  environment = "production"
}

output "gcs_bucket_url" {
  value = module.gcs_bucket.bucket_url
}
```

Components of a Module Block

Module Block: The module block begins and ends with {} and is used to call and configure a module within your Terraform configuration.

Module Name: gcs_bucket is the unique name for this module instance. This name is used to reference the module's outputs and resources elsewhere in the Terraform configuration.

Block Body: Within the {} braces, you specify arguments for the module. These arguments include the following:

- **source**: (required) This specifies the source of the module, which could be a local path, a Git repository, or a module registry.

- **input variables**: These correspond to variables defined in the module's variables.tf file. In the example, bucket_name, location, and environment are input variables.

- **version**: (recommended for registry modules) This specifies the version of the module to use. For example: version = "1.0.0".

- **Meta-Arguments**: Terraform provides additional optional meta-arguments that have special purposes:

  - count: Creates multiple instances of a module from a single module block.

  - for_each: Also creates multiple instances, but allows more control by iterating over a map or set of values.

  - providers: Passes specific provider configurations to a child module, useful when a module relies on different provider settings.

  - depends_on: Creates explicit dependencies between the module and other resources, ensuring Terraform processes them in the correct order.

Building a Module

Building a module in Terraform involves creating a reusable and self-contained configuration that manages resources in a modular way. Terraform modules follow a standard structure, which helps in generating documentation, indexing in module registries, and more.

Essential Elements of a Terraform Module

> **Root Module**: The main entry point of the module, typically containing Terraform files like main.tf, variables.tf, outputs.tf, and providers.tf. This is the only required element.

> **Resource Definitions**: The core of the module that defines the infrastructure resources.

> **Variables**: Define inputs that allow the customization of the module's behavior.

Outputs: Define outputs to expose values after the module is applied. All variables and outputs should have one or two sentence descriptions that explain their purposes.

Provider Configuration: Specifies the providers required by the module.

Documentation: A README.md file that describes the module, its inputs, outputs, and usage.

Sub-Modules: If necessary, a module can call other modules, creating complex setups through nested modules.

Minimal Module Structure

A minimal module might look like this:

```
$ tree minimal-module/
.
├── README.md
├── main.tf
├── variables.tf
├── outputs.tf
```

Example: Building a GCP Storage Bucket Module

It's time to do some practice!

Here I will show you how to build a module like the previous one step-by-step.

Step 1: Create Directory Structure

```
gcp_storage_bucket/
├── main.tf
├── variables.tf
```

```
├── outputs.tf
├── providers.tf
└── README.md
```

```
# in terminal

mkdir gcp_storage_bucket
cd gcp_storage_bucket
touch main.tf variables.tf outputs.tf providers.tf README.md
```

Step 2: Define Resources in Configuration File (main.tf)

```
resource "google_storage_bucket" "bucket" {
  name          = var.bucket_name
  location      = var.location
  storage_class = var.storage_class

  lifecycle_rule {
    action {
      type = "Delete"
    }
    condition {
      age = var.lifecycle_age
    }
  }

  versioning {
    enabled = var.versioning
  }

  labels = var.labels
}
```

Step 3: Define Input Variables (variables.tf)

```
variable "credentials_file_path" {
  description = "The path to the GCP credentials file"
  type        = string
}

variable "project_id" {
  description = "The GCP project ID"
  type        = string
}

variable "region" {
  description = "The region where resources will be created"
  type        = string
  default     = "us-west1"
}

variable "bucket_name" {
  description = "The name of the storage bucket"
  type        = string
}

variable "location" {
  description = "The location of the storage bucket"
  type        = string
  default     = "US"
}

variable "storage_class" {
  description = "The storage class of the bucket"
  type        = string
  default     = "STANDARD"
}
```

```
variable "lifecycle_age" {
  description = "The age of objects to be deleted"
  type        = number
  default     = 30
}

variable "versioning" {
  description = "Enable versioning"
  type        = bool
  default     = false
}

variable "labels" {
  description = "A map of labels to assign to the bucket"
  type        = map(string)
  default     = {}
}
```

Step 4: Define Outputs (outputs.tf)

```
output "bucket_name" {
  description = "The name of the storage bucket"
  value       = google_storage_bucket.bucket.name
}

output "bucket_self_link" {
  description = "The self link of the storage bucket"
  value       = google_storage_bucket.bucket.self_link
}

output "bucket_url" {
  description = "The URL of the storage bucket"
  value       = google_storage_bucket.bucket.url
}
```

Step 5: Define Provider Configuration (providers.tf)

```
terraform {
  required_providers {
    google = {
      source  = "hashicorp/google"
      version = "5.38.0"
    }
  }
}

provider "google" {
  credentials = file(var.credentials_file_path)
  project     = var.project_id
  region      = var.region
}
```

Step 6: Add a README.md File

Creating a README.md file is essential for documenting your Terraform module, as it provides clear instructions and examples for how to use the module effectively. This documentation makes your module easier to understand, reuse, and integrate into other projects.

```
# GCP Storage Bucket Module

# This Terraform module creates a Google Cloud Storage bucket
with customizable configurations.

module "bucket" {
  source                = "./gcp_storage_bucket"
  credentials_file_path = "/path/to/credentials.json"
  project_id            = "my-gcp-project"
  bucket_name           = "my-storage-bucket"
  location              = "US"
```

```
  storage_class      = "STANDARD"
  lifecycle_age      = 30
  versioning         = false
  labels             = {
    environment = "production"
  }
}
```

Inputs

Name	Description	Type	Default	Required
credentials_ file_path	The path to the GCP credentials file	string	n/a	yes
project_id	The GCP project ID	string	n/a	yes
region	The region where resources will be created	string	"us-west1"	no
bucket_name	The name of the storage bucket	string	n/a	yes
location	The location of the storage bucket	string	"US"	no
storage_ class	The storage class of the bucket	string	"STANDARD"	no
lifecycle_ age	The age of objects to be deleted	number	30	no
versioning	Enable versioning	bool	0	no
labels	A map of labels to assign to the bucket	map(string)	{}	no

Outputs

Name	Description
bucket_name	The name of the storage bucket
bucket_self_link	The self link of the storage bucket
bucket_url	The URL of the storage bucket

In this module, the inputs and outputs are defined clearly, making it easy for others to use and reuse in the future. A complete module in industry often contains nested modules and examples, along with comprehensive documentation and testing frameworks to ensure reliability and ease of integration.

Nested Modules

In complex infrastructure setups, you might need to structure your Terraform code using nested modules. A nested module is a module that is called from within another module. This allows you to break down your infrastructure into smaller, more manageable pieces, which can be organized hierarchically.

Example of Nested Modules

Suppose you're building an infrastructure setup that includes a network and a compute instance. Instead of defining everything in a single module, you can split them into separate submodules for better modularity and reuse:

```
module "network" {
  source = "./modules/network"
  network_name = "example-network"
  subnets = ["subnet-1", "subnet-2"]
}
```

```
module "compute" {
  source = "./modules/compute"
  instance_name = "example-instance"
  network = module.network.network_id
}
```

In this example, the network module is responsible for creating the necessary VPC and subnet configurations. The compute module depends on the network module and creates a virtual machine instance within the network created by the network module.

Organizing Nested Modules

Nested modules should be organized in a way that makes them easy to find and understand. Typically, they are placed in a modules/ directory within the root module.

```
$ tree complete-module/
.
├── README.md
├── main.tf
├── variables.tf
├── outputs.tf
├── ...
├── modules/
│   ├── nestedA/
│   │   ├── README.md
│   │   ├── variables.tf
│   │   ├── main.tf
│   │   ├── outputs.tf
│   ├── nestedB/
│   ├── .../
```

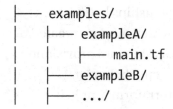

```
├── examples/
│    ├── exampleA/
│    │    ├── main.tf
│    ├── exampleB/
│    ├── .../
```

An `examples/` directory is essential for showcasing how your module can be used in real-world scenarios. Example configurations help users understand how to integrate the module into their own environments.

In industry-standard Terraform modules, it's important to go beyond just code. A well-documented module with clear examples and support for nested modules can significantly improve the maintainability and scalability of your Terraform infrastructure. By organizing your Terraform code into reusable, nested modules and providing thorough documentation, you create a robust foundation that can be easily adapted to various projects and environments. This approach not only saves time but also helps you and your team work more efficiently and confidently as your infrastructure evolves.

Dependencies

Now that you've established a strong foundation with well-structured modules, let's shift our focus to a new and critical topic: dependencies.

The concept of dependencies might seem straightforward at first, but it's actually the backbone of how Terraform orchestrates your infrastructure. When I first encountered the term, I was struck by how perfectly it captures the essence of interconnectedness in both code and life. Just like in the real world, where relationships can be financial or emotional dependencies, in Terraform, resources often rely on each other to exist and function correctly.

In Terraform, dependencies represent the relationships between resources or modules that determine the order in which they are created or modified. These dependencies ensure that your resources are provisioned in a logical sequence, preventing errors and unexpected behavior.

There are two main types of dependencies in Terraform: implicit dependencies and explicit dependencies.

Implicit Dependencies

Implicit dependencies are automatically recognized by Terraform based on how resources reference each other. For example, if one resource uses an attribute from another, Terraform knows that it needs to create the second resource first.

```
provider "google" {
  project = "terraform-made-easy"
  region  = "us-central1"
}

resource "google_compute_network" "default" {
  name = "default-network"
}

resource "google_compute_instance" "default" {
  name         = "vm-instance"
  machine_type = "n1-standard-1"
  zone         = "us-central1-a"

  boot_disk {
    initialize_params {
      image = "debian-cloud/debian-11"
    }
  }
}
```

```
network_interface {
  network = google_compute_network.default.self_link
}
}
```

Here, the google_compute_instance.default resource has an implicit dependency on google_compute_network.default because it references the network's self_link. Terraform automatically ensures the network is created before the instance, without you needing to specify this relationship.

Inspect the Dependency

If you want to see an intuitive and simplified graph that describes only the dependency ordering of the resources, you can use the terraform graph command. Here is an example, which creates a graph for applying the given plan and stores the graph in your working directory:

```
$ terraform graph -type=plan | dot -Tpng >graph.png
```

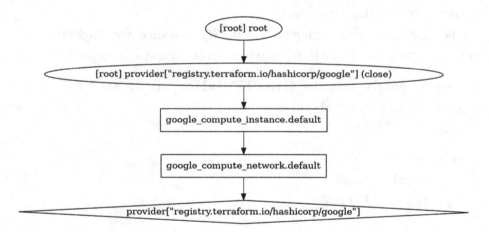

Figure 3-2. *Visualizing Resource Dependencies with Terraform Graph*

The arrows indicate the dependency hierarchy. The google_compute_
network.default must be created before the google_compute_instance.
default, as networks are often prerequisites for instances. The
dependency arrow from google_compute_instance.default to google_
compute_network.default shows that the instance relies on the network
for network connectivity.

There are plenty of examples of implicit dependencies in GCP, and you'll
encounter many more in the next chapter. For instance, a subnet implicitly
depends on the VPC it belongs to, a firewall rule on the security group it's
associated with, and an instance on the boot disk it's attached to. These
dependencies are automatically recognized by Terraform, ensuring your
infrastructure is built in the correct order without you having to lift a finger.

Explicit Dependencies

Sometimes, dependencies aren't as obvious to Terraform. When you
need to enforce a specific order, you can use the depends_on argument to
explicitly declare the dependency.

For instance, when setting up a cloud SQL instance, you might want to
ensure that a firewall rule is in place before the database is created.

```
resource "google_compute_firewall" "allow_sql_access" {
  name    = "allow-sql-access"
  network = "default"

  allow {
    protocol = "tcp"
    ports    = ["3306"]
  }

  source_ranges = ["0.0.0.0/0"] # Adjust this to
  restrict access
}
```

```
resource "google_sql_database_instance" "my_database" {
  name             = "my-database"
  database_version = "POSTGRES_14"
  region           = "us-west1"

  # ... Other database configuration

  depends_on = [google_compute_firewall.allow_sql_access]
}
```

In this example, the database instance won't be created until the firewall rule is in place, thanks to the depends_on argument.

Module Dependencies

Module dependencies refer to situations where one module relies on resources created by another module before it can function correctly. Terraform doesn't have a built-in mechanism for direct module dependencies, but you can achieve them using a combination of input variables and output values.

Imagine you have two modules: one called vpc_module that creates a VPC network and subnet, and another called webserver_module that provisions a web server within that VPC. The webserver_module needs information about the VPC and subnet from the vpc_module.

```
#Define output in vpc_module

output "vpc_network" {
  value = google_compute_network.main.name
}
output "subnet_name" {
  value = google_compute_subnetwork.public.name
}
```

And then define input variables to accept these values and use them in the instance configuration in the webserver_module.

```
variable "vpc_network" {
  type = string
}

variable "subnet_name" {
  type = string
}

resource "google_compute_instance" "web_server" {
  name         = "my-web-server"
  machine_type = "e2-micro"

  network_interface {
    network = var.vpc_network
    subnetwork = "projects/your-project-id/regions/region-name/
    subnetworks/" + var.subnet_name
  }

  depends_on = [google_compute_subnetwork.public]
}
```

By using input variables and output values, you can create a dependency between the modules. Terraform ensures the vpc_module is applied first, so the necessary networking information is available when webserver_module is provisioned.

While dependencies might seem like a minor detail, mastering them can elevate your Terraform skills to a new level. By understanding and leveraging dependencies, you're not just ensuring that your infrastructure is built in a reliable, predictable way; you're also setting the stage for smooth deployments, efficient management, and a more resilient infrastructure.

Infrastructure Management

Terraform excels at defining and provisioning infrastructure through configuration files, but a key aspect of its functionality involves tracking the resources it creates and managing their ongoing state. Understanding how Terraform handles the creation, reading, updating, and deletion (CRUD) of resources, as well as how it stores and uses metadata, is essential.

Let's delve deeper into these processes with detailed explanations and examples.

Understanding State

Terraform keeps track of your infrastructure using a concept called `state`. Think of the state as a map that connects your real-world resources to the configurations defined in your Terraform files.It also stores additional information about these resources and helps Terraform work more efficiently, especially for large setups. By default, Terraform stores this state in a local file named `terraform.tfstate`.

State serves several important functions:

- **Mapping**: It links physical resources with their configuration.

- **Efficiency**: It helps Terraform work more efficiently, especially in larger setups.

- **Change Management**: It records the identity of remote objects created and helps Terraform update or remove these resources based on future changes.

Here's a simplified view of a `terraform.tfstate` file, which is a JSON document containing the state of your infrastructure:

```
{
  "version": 4,
  "terraform_version": "1.5.7",
  "serial": 25,
  "lineage": "d09d80a0-7d6f-4f5c-bb4d-62aeb631d396",
  "outputs": {},
  "resources": [],
  "check_results": null
}
```

> **version:** It specifies the version of the state file format. Terraform uses it to understand how to read and write state files.
>
> **terraform_version:** It indicates the version of Terraform that was used to create or last modify the state file. It helps in ensuring compatibility and debugging.
>
> **serial:** It is an incrementing counter that increases with each modification of the state file.
>
> **lineage:** It is a unique identifier for the state file, generated when the state file is first created. It remains constant across all versions of the state file, even as the serial number increases. This identifier helps in ensuring that state files can be uniquely identified, especially when working with remote backends or when migrating state files.

outputs: It contains output values from your Terraform configurations. In this case, it's an empty object, indicating that there are no outputs defined in the Terraform configuration.

resources: This field lists all the resources that Terraform is managing. Each resource includes details such as its type, name, properties, and metadata. Here, it's an empty array, meaning there are no resources currently managed by this state file.

check_results: This field is used to store the results of any checks that have been run. It's null here, indicating that no checks have been performed or no results have been recorded.

This structured approach allows Terraform to manage your infrastructure state efficiently and ensures that changes are applied in a predictable and error-free manner.

Local State and Remote State

There are two main approaches to storing Terraform state: local and remote. Choosing the right approach depends on your specific needs.

Local State

Local state refers to storing the state file on your local machine's filesystem, typically in the same directory where you run Terraform commands. This is the default approach. When you initialize Terraform (`terraform init`) or run subsequent commands, a file named `terraform.tfstate` is automatically created and managed in your working directory.

Local state offers a straightforward approach with easy setup (no configuration needed) and the convenience of hands-on access for inspection. However, its limitations become apparent in collaborative environments: it lacks conflict resolution for multiple users, increases data loss risk due to the absence of automatic backups, and exposes sensitive data with less robust security compared to encrypted remote backends. As such, local state is best suited for solo users or initial experimentation with Terraform.

Remote State

Remote state involves storing the Terraform state file in a remote backend. Remote backends can be a variety of storage services, such as AWS S3, Azure Blob Storage, Google Cloud Storage, HashiCorp Consul, Terraform Cloud, and others.

Here's an example of configuring GCS as a remote back end:

```
terraform {
  backend "gcs" {
    bucket = "my-terraform-state-bucket"
    key    = "path/to/my/key"
    region = "us-west1"
  }
}
```

While remote state introduces some complexity through additional configuration and potential storage costs, it offers significant advantages for teams. These include maintaining a single source of truth for infrastructure through collaboration, preventing data inconsistencies with state locking mechanisms, enhanced security features like encryption and access controls, and built-in backup and recovery functionalities offered by many remote backends.

For larger projects or collaborative environments, remote backends are generally preferred due to their support for multiple users and versioning. You will see the detailed example in the next chapter.

Understanding Back Ends

In Terraform, a back end is a configuration block that specifies how Terraform should store its state data. Terraform state is a mapping of resources that allows Terraform to manage the infrastructure. The back-end configuration determines where this state data is stored and how it is accessed.

There are two types of back ends:

Local Back End

It stores the state file on the local filesystem.

This is suitable for small projects or testing purposes.

```
terraform {
  backend "local" {
    path = "/path/to/terraform.tfstate"
  }
}
```

Remote Backend

It stores the state file on remote storage services such as AWS S3, Google Cloud Storage, Azure Blob Storage, and others.

```
terraform {
  backend "gcs" {
    bucket = "my-terraform-state-bucke"
    prefix = "terraform/state"
  }
}
```

Terraform back ends are like safe deposit boxes for your infrastructure. They let multiple people work on the same infrastructure setup (called its *state*) without accidentally stepping on each other's toes. Backends also keep track of changes to your infrastructure over time, just like version control keeps track of changes to your code. And if something goes wrong, having a backup of your state in a remote location means you can easily get things back up and running. As such, for larger projects or collaborative environments, it's best to use a remote back end.

Managing Workspaces

Imagine you work at a large company building a web application that needs to be deployed across multiple environments: development (dev), staging, and production (prod). Initially, you might set up separate Terraform configurations for each environment, duplicating most of the code. While this approach works, it quickly becomes cumbersome. Managing state files for each configuration becomes challenging, and manually switching environments can lead to errors.

This is where Terraform workspaces come into play. Workspaces in Terraform allow you to manage multiple environments—such as development, staging, and production—within a single configuration. Each workspace maintains its own state file, ensuring that changes in one environment do not unintentionally impact another. This separation is crucial for preventing accidental modifications in production while working on development or staging environments.

Terraform includes a default workspace named default, but you can create and switch between custom workspaces by using the terraform workspace command.

```
# Create a workspace for development environment
 terraform workspace new dev
```

```
# Switch to the dev workspace
terraform workspace select dev
```

Workspaces simplify managing different environments and significantly reduce the need for duplicating Terraform configurations, making it easier to manage infrastructure across multiple stages and maintain a consistent deployment process.

Understanding State Locking

Imagine two developers working on a company website using Terraform. One is updating the server capacity to handle a traffic surge, while the other is removing an unused database. If both attempt to apply changes simultaneously, they risk causing conflicts and inconsistencies. This is where Terraform's state locking mechanism comes into play.

What Is State Locking?

Locking in Terraform is a mechanism to prevent concurrent operations on the same set of resources, which can help avoid conflicts and ensure consistency. It acts like a digital handshake, ensuring only one person can make changes to the Terraform code at a time, preventing these conflicts and keeping your infrastructure stable. This is especially important in collaborative environments or when using CI/CD pipelines.

How State Locking Works

The primary focus of state locking is the Terraform state file. When using a remote back end for your Terraform state—such as Google Cloud Storage (GCS)—Terraform can automatically lock the state file to prevent other processes from making simultaneous changes. This ensures that updates to the infrastructure are applied smoothly and without conflict.

For example, when applying a Terraform configuration:

```
# google_compute_instance.default will be created
+ resource "google_compute_instance" "default" {
    # ...
  }
```

Plan: 1 to add, 0 to change, 0 to destroy.

Terraform locks the state file in the remote back end, like this:

```
Do you want to perform these actions in workspace "default"?
  Terraform will write the state for this workspace to
  "gs://my-terraform-state-bucket/terraform/state/default/
  terraform.tfstate"
  Enter a value: yes
```

After applying the changes:

```
google_compute_instance.default: Creating...
google_compute_instance.default: Creation complete after 31s
[id=terraform-instance]

Apply complete! Resources: 1 added, 0 changed, 0 destroyed.
```

The lock is automatically released once the operation is complete, allowing others to proceed with their changes.

Manual Unlocking

In some cases, you may need to manually unlock the state file if a previous operation was interrupted and left a lock in place. You need to find the lock ID from the error message and then use the terraform force-unlock command to unlock the state.

```
$ terraform force-unlock LOCK_ID
```

However, manual unlocking should be approached with care. Unlocking the state while someone else is still holding the lock can lead to conflicts or corruption. Use force-unlock only if you're certain that the lock was left by a failed operation and no one else is actively working on the state.

By understanding and properly managing state locking, you can ensure that your Terraform workflows remain smooth and reliable, even in a collaborative setting.

Summary

This chapter was dense with information, covering a range of new concepts, terms, and definitions. It's perfectly normal if you're feeling a bit overwhelmed—learning often involves a winding path with ups and downs. But remember, every challenge brings you closer to mastery.

In this chapter, we delved into several critical aspects of Terraform. We started with an overview of versatile providers, variables, and outputs. We then explored how to build and organize modules effectively. Understanding the relationships between resources and leveraging dependency management was a key focus, aimed at provisioning more resilient infrastructure.

We also covered essential infrastructure management topics such as state files, backends, workspaces, and locking mechanisms. These tools and settings are designed to enhance consistency, convenience, and efficiency in your Terraform workflows.

As you continue to explore and practice, you'll uncover the elegance and logic embedded in Terraform's approach. The more you engage with these concepts, the more you'll appreciate the depth and functionality they offer.

Keep going—your efforts will lead to a deeper understanding and greater mastery of Terraform. In the next chapter, we'll shift gears and dive into hands-on practices to solidify your knowledge and skills.

CHAPTER 4

Provisioning Infrastructure on GCP

Now that you have a solid understanding of Terraform's theoretical concepts, it's time to put that knowledge into practice! In this chapter, you will dive into using Terraform to provision and manage infrastructure on Google Cloud Platform (GCP). You'll start with foundational elements like Cloud Storage, Compute Engine, and Virtual Private Cloud (VPC) to help you build a basic cloud environment. As you progress, you'll explore more advanced topics, including Cloud SQL, service accounts, and Google Kubernetes Engine (GKE).

Through practical, hands-on examples, you'll reinforce the concepts covered in previous chapters. The exercises on foundational infrastructure will equip you with the skills to efficiently provision and configure cloud environments. Meanwhile, the advanced examples will guide you in avoiding common pitfalls, enhancing code quality, and achieving complex goals such as high availability, granular access control, and robust security management.

Provisioning Cloud Storage

Cloud Storage is a fundamental infrastructure component on Google Cloud Platform (GCP). In this section, you'll begin by creating a simple Cloud Storage bucket to help you understand the basic concepts. Then, you'll explore how to use variables and Terraform functions to efficiently

© Ivy Wang 2024
I. Wang, *Terraform Made Easy*, https://doi.org/10.1007/979-8-8688-1010-7_4

create and manage multiple bucket resources. Finally, you'll learn how to configure Cloud Storage for state management, including setting up Terraform back ends and migrating your back end from a local environment to a remote one. This will ensure your infrastructure's state is securely stored and easily accessible for future updates.

Create a Storage Bucket

This is our first hands-on example in the book, so let me guide beginners who may be new to GCP through the process.

Once you're logged in to your Google Cloud Platform console, you can activate the Cloud Shell. From there, use the command `touch main.tf` to create a new configuration file.

Figure 4-1. *Creating a Terraform Configuration File in the Cloud Shell Environment*

Then, you can click the Open Editor button, open the `main.tf` file, and write the configuration code as shown here:

```
terraform {
  required_providers {
    google = {
```

```
      source = "hashicorp/google"
      version = "5.38.0"
    }
  }
}

provider "google" {
  project = "terraform-made-easy"  #replace to your project id
  region  = "us-central1"
  zone    = "us-central1-a"
}

resource "google_storage_bucket" "default" {
  name          = "ivys_bucket_a"  # give your unique
bucket name
  location      = "US"
  storage_class = "STANDARD"
}
```

The first block is the terraform block, and inside it is the required_
provider block, which defines the provider (google) and source
(hashicorp/google) and specifies the version of the provider plugin to use.

The second block is the provider block, containing the necessary
details to authenticate and manage resources in GCP. A region can have
multiple zones (a zone is where resources will be created).

The third block is the resource block, which specifies a Google Cloud
Storage bucket resource will be created.

default is the name of this resource instance. It is an arbitrary name
used to reference this resource within the configuration. The bucket
name must be globally unique. The location refers to where the resource
will be created physically. The US means the bucket will be created in a
multiregion location in the United States.

The STANDARD is the default storage class offering low-latency access to
frequently accessed data.

You can save the changes by pressing Ctrl+S.

If you are new to configuration files, it's common for your formatting to become a bit disorganized, with misaligned code and inconsistent spacing. To fix this, you can use the `terraform fmt` command. This tool automatically formats your `.tf` files, ensuring they are clean, well-organized, and easy to read. Proper formatting also helps to reduce errors and makes the code easier to maintain.

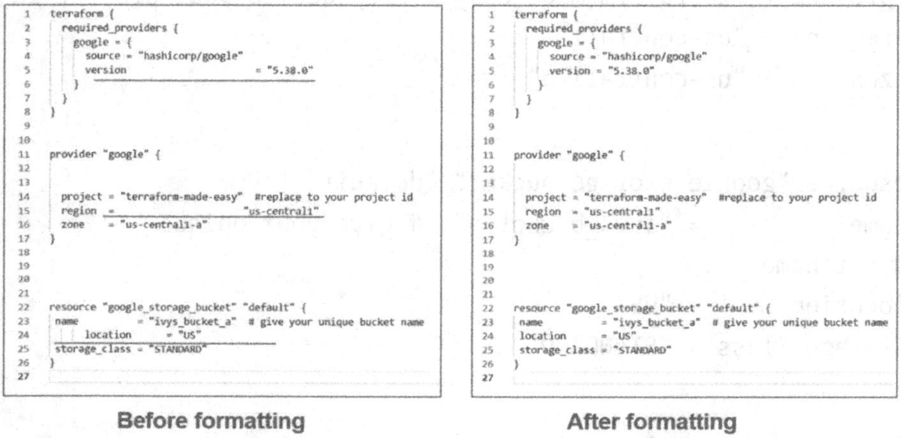

Before formatting   After formatting

Figure 4-2. *Comparison of Code Formatting Before and After Applying Terraform Format*

Let's move to the Cloud Shell to start working with Terraform. Before anything else, you need to initialize Terraform using the command `terraform init`. This command sets up your Terraform environment by initializing the back end and downloading the necessary provider plugins. Here's what you might see:

```
Initializing the backend...

Initializing provider plugins...
- Finding hashicorp/google versions matching "5.38.0"...
- Installing hashicorp/google v5.38.0...
- Installed hashicorp/google v5.38.0 (signed by HashiCorp)
```

Terraform has made some changes to the provider dependency selections recorded in the .terraform.lock.hcl file. Review those changes and commit them to your version control system if they represent changes you intended to make.

Terraform has been successfully initialized!

After initialization, the next step is to generate an execution plan. It's a good practice to save this plan using the -out option. This option creates a binary file that contains all the actions Terraform will take to reach the desired state of your infrastructure. In this example, the execution plan is saved to a file named plan.out.

```
$ terraform plan -out=plan.out
```

Terraform used the selected providers to generate the following execution plan. Resource actions are indicated with the following symbols:
  + create

Terraform will perform the following actions:

```
  # google_storage_bucket.default will be created
  + resource "google_storage_bucket" "default" {
      + effective_labels          = (known after apply)
      + force_destroy             = false
      + id                        = (known after apply)
      + location                  = "US"
      + name                      = "ivys_bucket_a"
      + project                   = (known after apply)
      + project_number            = (known after apply)
      + public_access_prevention  = (known after apply)
      + rpo                       = (known after apply)
```

```
    + self_link                        = (known after apply)
    + storage_class                    = "STANDARD"
    + terraform_labels                 = (known after apply)
    + uniform_bucket_level_access      = (known after apply)
    + url                              = (known after apply)
  }

Plan: 1 to add, 0 to change, 0 to destroy.
```

Saved the plan to: plan.out

Now you can use this plan file as input to the terraform apply command. This approach ensures that Terraform will execute the exact set of actions proposed by the plan, without recalculating or modifying the plan. This is especially important because if the infrastructure changes after the plan is generated, rerunning terraform plan could yield a different result.

```
$  terraform apply "plan.out"
```

```
google_storage_bucket.default: Creating...
google_storage_bucket.default: Creation complete after 1s
[id=ivys_bucket_a]
```

Apply complete! Resources: 1 added, 0 changed, 0 destroyed.

Confirming Resource Creation

After executing the Terraform plan, you can verify that the Google Cloud Storage bucket has been created as expected. There are two primary methods to do this:

Google Cloud Console: You can manually check the details of the bucket. Navigate to the Storage section, find the bucket named ivys_bucket_a, and review its configuration to confirm that it matches what was defined in your Terraform files.

Command Line: Using the Google Cloud gcloud command-line tool is often a quicker and more automated way to verify the creation of resources. To check the details of the bucket, run the following command:

```
$ gcloud storage buckets describe gs://ivys_bucket_a
```

This command retrieves and displays the details of the bucket named ivys_bucket_a. By reviewing this information, you can confirm that the bucket matches the configuration specified in your Terraform files and that everything was set up according to your expectations.

Create Multiple Storage Buckets

In this section, you will explore how to use variables and functions to create and manage multiple resources simultaneously, ensuring consistency and saving time.

In this example, you will create three storage buckets in the same region with different names.

```
provider "google" {
  project = "terraform-made-easy"
  region  = "us-central1"
  # credentials = file("path/to/your/service-account-key.json")
}
```

```
# Variables
variable "bucket_names" {
  type        = list(string)
  description = "A list of names for the Google Cloud Storage
                buckets to be created."
  default     = ["ivys_bucket_1", "ivys_bucket_2",
                "ivys_bucket_3"]
}

variable "location" {
  type        = string
  description = "The geographic location where the storage
                buckets will be created."
  default     = "us-central1"
}

variable "storage_class" {
  type        = string
  description = "The storage class to be assigned to the
                buckets (e.g., STANDARD, NEARLINE)."
  default     = "STANDARD"
}

# Resource Definition
resource "google_storage_bucket" "buckets" {
  count = length(var.bucket_names)

  name          = var.bucket_names[count.index]
  location      = var.location
  storage_class = var.storage_class
}
```

The first block in the configuration is the `provider` block. In this block, you'll notice a line for credentials that has been commented out. This is because, in this scenario, you're using the Google Cloud environment directly, which handles authentication automatically.

However, if you're not using Google Cloud SDK authentication or working directly within a Google Cloud environment, you'll need to specify the credentials explicitly. This credentials line points to a service account key file, which provides Terraform with the necessary authentication to manage Google Cloud resources. For more details on how to set up and use credentials with Terraform on Google Cloud, you can refer to the `documentation on authentication`.

Following the provider block, you have three variable blocks that define key configuration settings The variable `bucket_names` defines a variable called `bucket_names`, which is a list of strings. The description explains that this variable will hold the names of the storage buckets to be created, making it clear and reader-friendly.The default value is a list containing `bucket1`, `bucket2`, and `bucket3`.

The last block is the resource block. Here, the `count` meta-argument is set to the length of the `bucket_names` list, which means that this resource block will be instantiated once for each bucket name provided. The `name` argument within the block dynamically sets the name of each bucket, using `count.index` to reference the corresponding element in the `bucket_names` list. This ensures that each bucket is uniquely named according to the values specified in the `bucket_names` variable. Later in this chapter, you will explore how to achieve similar results using the `for_each` meta-argument, which offers additional flexibility and control.

You can apply the configuration in the terminal by using command `terraform apply` and observe the results.

```
Only 'yes' will be accepted to approve.

  Enter a value: yes

google_storage_bucket.buckets[0]: Creating...
google_storage_bucket.buckets[2]: Creating...
google_storage_bucket.buckets[1]: Creating...
google_storage_bucket.buckets[0]: Creation complete after 2s [id=ivys_bucket_1]
google_storage_bucket.buckets[1]: Creation complete after 2s [id=ivys_bucket_2]
google_storage_bucket.buckets[2]: Creation complete after 2s [id=ivys_bucket_3]

Apply complete! Resources: 3 added, 0 changed, 0 destroyed.
ivyvan_w@cloudshell:~/terraform/storage_buckets (instruction-415216)$
```

Figure 4-3. *Creating Multiple Storage Buckets Using Terraform*

If you want to change the variable values manually, you can execute
the configuration with additional settings.

For example, in this case, the location will be changed from the
default value of us-central1 to us-youst1 and the storage _class will be
changed to NEARLINE.

```
terraform apply -var='bucket_names=["ivys_bucket1", "ivys_
bucket2", "ivys_bucket3"]' -var='location=us-youst1'
-var='storage_class=NEARLINE'
```

	Name ↑	Created	Location type	Location	Default storage class ❓
☐	instruction-415216-data	6 May 2024, 13:45:38	Region	europe-west3	Standard
☐	ivys_bucket1	27 May 2024, 17:17:15	Region	us-west1	Nearline
☐	ivys_bucket2	27 May 2024, 17:17:15	Region	us-west1	Nearline
☐	ivys_bucket3	27 May 2024, 17:17:15	Region	us-west1	Nearline

Figure 4-4. *Updating Variable Values in a Terraform Configuration*

Google Cloud Storage for State Management

Terraform uses a state file to keep track of the resources it manages. A common approach for managing Terraform state is to store it in a remote back end, such as Google Cloud Storage (GCS). This allows multiple team members to collaborate on the same infrastructure and ensures that the state is consistently stored and available.

Create a Cloud Storage Bucket for Remote State

The first step is to create a storage bucket to hold the Terraform state. This can be accomplished using the gcloud command or directly through Terraform, depending on your preference.

Option 1: Create a GCS bucket with the gcloud command.

```
gcloud storage buckets create gs://ivys-terraformf-state-bucket
```

Option 2: Create a GCS bucket in Terraform.

```
# create storage bucket
resource "google_storage_bucket" "state-bucket" {
  name          = "ivys-terraform-state-bucket"
  location      = "US"
  storage_class = "STANDARD"
}
```

Configure the Terraform Back End

Second, you need to configure the Terraform back end in the main.tf file.

```
terraform {
  backend "gcs" {
    bucket  = "my-terraform-state-bucket"
```

```
    prefix = "terraform/state"
  }
}
```

Terraform integrates seamlessly with Google Cloud Storage (GCS) to support state locking, a crucial feature that prevents concurrent operations from potentially corrupting the Terraform state file—a key element in managing your infrastructure. The state file acts as a record of the resources managed by Terraform, ensuring that the desired state is aligned with the actual state of your infrastructure. GCS enhances state locking by utilizing its object versioning feature. Object versioning in GCS allows multiple versions of an object (such as the Terraform state file) to coexist within a bucket. By enabling versioning on your GCS bucket, every change to the state file is preserved as a distinct version. This feature not only provides a safety net against corruption or accidental deletion but also makes it easier to revert to a previous state if needed, thereby ensuring robust and reliable infrastructure management.

```
resource "google_storage_bucket" "state-bucket" {
  name          = "ivys-terraform-state-bucket"
  location      = "US"
  storage_class = "STANDARD"

  force_destroy             = false
  public_access_prevention  = "enforced"
  uniform_bucket_level_access = true

  versioning {
    enabled = true
  }
}
```

In this example, setting `location` = `"US"` designates the bucket as multiregional, meaning that data is redundantly stored across multiple regions within the United States. This setup enhances both availability and reliability. The `force_destroy` = `false` configuration ensures that the bucket cannot be deleted forcefully, especially if it contains objects, thus preventing accidental data loss. The `public_access_prevention` = `"enforced"` setting provides robust security by safeguarding the bucket against unintentional or malicious public access. By enabling `uniform_bucket_level_access` = `true`, all access permissions are managed uniformly at the bucket level, which simplifies permission management. Finally, enabling `versioning` allows each change to an object (such as the Terraform state file) to be stored as a distinct version. This feature is invaluable for tracking changes and recovering from accidental deletions or data corruption.

The full `main.tf` is as follows:

```
terraform {
  backend "gcs" {
    bucket  = "my-terraform-state-bucket"
    prefix  = "terraform/state"
  }
}

provider "google" {
  project = "project ID"
  region  = "us-central1"
}

resource "google_storage_bucket" "state-bucket" {
  name            = "ivys-terraform-state-bucket"
  location        = "US"
  storage_class   = "STANDARD"
```

```
force_destroy               = false
public_access_prevention    = "enforced"
uniform_bucket_level_access = true

versioning {
    enabled = true
  }
}
```

Migrate the Back End from Local to Remote

Migrating the Terraform back end from a local environment to a remote one is a common and important task, especially as your infrastructure grows and requires more robust state management. This process involves updating your Terraform configuration to specify the new remote back end, initializing the back end, and migrating your existing state to the remote storage.

Step 1: Update Terraform Configuration

The first step is to modify your Terraform configuration file (usually main.tf or backend.tf) to define the new back end. In this example, you'll migrate to a Google Cloud Storage (GCS) back end. The updated configuration will look like this:

```
terraform {
  backend "gcs" {
    bucket  = "my-terraform-state-bucket"
    prefix  = "terraform/state"
  }
}
```

Step 2: Initialize the New Back End

Once the configuration is updated, run `terraform init` to initialize Terraform with the new back end configuration.

Terraform will recognize that the back end has changed and will prompt you to confirm the migration of your existing state from local storage to the GCS bucket. You will need to specify yes to proceed with the migration. During this process, Terraform securely copies your current state file to the specified remote back end.

Step 3: Verify the Migration

To verify the migration, you can run `terraform init` again to confirm Terraform is using the GCS back end. This time, Terraform should not prompt you to migrate the state, indicating that it is now properly using the GCS back end.

Step 4: Manually Migrate the Existing State

If you already have a state file that you need to migrate manually, Terraform provides commands to facilitate this process. First, pull the current state from the local back end. This command saves the current state to a file named terraform.tfstate.

Next, push this state to the new GCS back end. This will transfer the state file to the remote back end, ensuring it is stored and managed by GCS moving forward.

```
terraform state pull > terraform.tfstate
terraform state push
```

Migrating the back end involves coordination across various services, so it's crucial to verify that you have the necessary IAM roles or service account permissions to access the GCS bucket. Additionally, if your local state file was encrypted using a custom key, ensure that it is decrypted before migrating to GCS. This will prevent any issues related to accessing or managing the state in the new environment.

Provision Compute Engines

Cloud Compute Engine is a core infrastructure component on GCP that lets you run virtual machines in the cloud. In this section, you'll start by creating a simple Compute Engine instance using Terraform. Then, you'll explore how to make this process more efficient by using loops to create multiple instances with ease. Additionally, you'll learn how to create and use modules in Terraform, which will demonstrate how to improve both the efficiency and flexibility of your infrastructure provisioning.

Create a Compute Engine

Google Compute Engine (GCE) is a vital component of Google Cloud Platform (GCP), offering robust virtual machines (VMs) that power a wide range of applications and services. Provisioning GCE VMs can often involve complex and repetitive tasks. ButTerraform simplifies the procedure.

Here is an example of provisioning a compute instance with a default network:

```
provider "google" {
  project = "terraform-made-easy"
  region  = "us-central1"
}

resource "google_compute_instance" "default" {
  name         = "my-instance"
  machine_type = "e2-medium"
```

```
boot_disk {
  initialize_params {
    image = "debian-cloud/debian-11"
  }
}
network_interface {
  network = "default"
  access_config {
    // Ephemeral public IP
  }
}
}
```

The resource block contains multiple properties that define various aspects of the virtual machine. First, it creates a compute instance resource named default with a custom name "my-instance". Then it specifies a machine type e2-medium, which defines the virtual CPU, memory, and storage for the instance.

The boot disk configures the storage for the instance. Second, it defines a boot disk that will be initialized using an image, which provides a Debian 11 operating system to be installed on the instance.

The network interface defines how the instance will connect to the network. In this case, it's set to default, which means an ephemeral public IP address will be created by GCP and assigned to the instance. The public IP address allows external machines to connect to your instance remotely.

```
$ terraform apply
```

```
Terraform used the selected providers to generate the following
execution plan. Resource actions are indicated with the
following symbols:
  + create
```

Terraform will perform the following actions:

```
  # google_compute_instance.default will be created
  + resource "google_compute_instance" "default" {
      + can_ip_forward        = false
      + cpu_platform          = (known after apply)
      + current_status        = (known after apply)
      + deletion_protection   = false
      + effective_labels      = (known after apply)
      + guest_accelerator     = (known after apply)
      + id                    = (known after apply)
      + instance_id           = (known after apply)
      + label_fingerprint     = (known after apply)
      + machine_type          = "e2-medium"
      + metadata_fingerprint  = (known after apply)
      + min_cpu_platform      = (known after apply)
      + name                  = "my-instance"
      + project               = "terraform-made-easy"
      + self_link             = (known after apply)
      + tags_fingerprint      = (known after apply)
      + terraform_labels      = (known after apply)
      + zone                  = "us-central1-a"

      + boot_disk {
          + auto_delete                = true
          + device_name                = (known after apply)
          + disk_encryption_key_sha256 = (known after apply)
          + kms_key_self_link          = (known after apply)
          + mode                       = "READ_WRITE"
          + source                     = (known after apply)

          + initialize_params {
              + image                      = "debian-cloud/
                                             debian-11"
```

```
            + labels                = (known after apply)
            + provisioned_iops      = (known after apply)
            + provisioned_throughput = (known after apply)
            + size                  = (known after apply)
            + type                  = (known after apply)
          }
      }

    + network_interface {
        + internal_ipv6_prefix_length = (known after apply)
        + ipv6_access_type          = (known after apply)
        + ipv6_address              = (known after apply)
        + name                      = (known after apply)
        + network                   = "default"
        + network_ip                = (known after apply)
        + stack_type                = (known after apply)
        + subnetwork                = (known after apply)
        + subnetwork_project        = (known after apply)

        + access_config {
            + nat_ip       = (known after apply)
            + network_tier = (known after apply)
          }
      }
  }

Plan: 1 to add, 0 to change, 0 to destroy.

Do you want to perform these actions?
  Terraform will perform the actions described above.
  Only 'yes' will be accepted to approve.

Enter a value: yes
```

```
google_compute_instance.default: Creating...
google_compute_instance.default: Still creating...
[10s elapsed]
google_compute_instance.default: Creation complete after 16s
[id=projects/terraform-made-easy/zones/us-central1-a/instances/
my-instance]
```

```
Apply complete! Resources: 1 added, 0 changed, 0 destroyed.
```

After execution, you can verify the results with the gcloud command. For example, if you want to get the basic information of the virtual machine such as name, zone, or status, you can use the following command with the --format flag:

```
$ gcloud compute instances describe my-instance --zone=us-
central1-a
--format="get(name,zone,status)"
```

```
my-instance      https://www.googleapis.com/compute/v1/projects/
terraform-made-easy/zones/us-central1-a    RUNNING
```

If you want to check the ephemeral external IP address, you can get it in this way:

```
$ gcloud compute instances describe my-instance
--zone=us-central1-a --format="get(networkInterfaces[0].
accessConfigs[0].natIP)"
```

```
34.45.33.154
```

In this case, the ephemeral external IP address is 34.45.33.154.

Create Multiple Compute Engines with Tags

When provisioning multiple compute instances with Terraform on Google Cloud Platform, you have two main approaches: leveraging modules or using loops with meta-arguments such as count or for_each. Each approach offers distinct advantages depending on the complexity and requirements of your infrastructure setup.

Modules in Terraform are reusable containers that encapsulate multiple resources and their configurations. They allow you to define a set of resources once and use them across various parts of your infrastructure or even across different projects. Modules help in organizing code, enhancing reusability, and maintaining consistency.

In this section, you will delve into the creation and utilization of modules. Consider a scenario where you need to deploy two compute instances on GCP, each with distinct tags. By using modules, you can encapsulate the configuration for each instance, allowing for consistent deployment while customizing specific aspects like tags for each instance.

We'll walk through the process of defining a module to create compute instances and then use that module to instantiate two compute instances with unique tags, demonstrating how modules can simplify and streamline your infrastructure management.

```
# tree structure of the terraform project
.
├── main.tf
└── modules
    └── compute_instance
        └── main.tf

3 directories, 2 files
```

This is a tree structure of the configuration directory. The root level consists of a `main.tf` file, which serves as the main configuration file for the `terraform` project, and a directory named `modules`, which may contain subdirectories for various modules.

Within the modules directory, there is another directory called `compute_instance`. Inside `compute_instance`, there is a `main.tf` file, which defines the resources and configuration for the `compute_instance` module.

Then let's move to the configuration file in the module. It defines several input variables such as `instance_name`, `machine_type`, `zone`, and `tags`.

Following the variable definitions is the resource block, which uses the previously defined input variables. This modular approach allows for easy reuse and customization across different parts of your infrastructure.

```
# module level configuration file

variable "instance_name" {
  description = "The name of the Compute Engine instance"
  type        = string
}

variable "machine_type" {
  description = "The machine type of the Compute Engine
                instance"
  type        = string
}

variable "zone" {
  description = "The zone in which the Compute Engine instance
                will be created"
  type        = string
}
```

```
variable "tags" {
  description = "A list of tags to apply to the Compute Engine
                instance"
  type        = list(string)
  default     = []
}

resource "google_compute_instance" "compute_instance" {
    name = var.instance_name
    machine_type = var.machine_type
    zone = var.zone

    boot_disk {
      initialize_params {
        image = "debian-cloud/debian-11"
      }
    }

    network_interface {
      network = "default"
      access_config {

      }
    }

    tags = var.tags
}
```

Next, you can focus on the project-level configuration file. This section of the code is concise and straightforward, as it mainly involves invoking the module twice and assigning values to the required variables.

```
# project level configuration file - main.tf

provider "google" {
  project = "terraform-made-easy"
```

```
  region = "us-central1"
}

module "instance1"{
    source = "./modules/compute_instance"
    instance_name = "instance-1"
    machine_type = "e2-medium"
    zone = "us-central1-a"
    tags = ["dev","web"]
}

module "instance2"{
    source = "./modules/compute_instance"
    instance_name = "instance-2"
    machine_type = "n1-standard-1"
    zone = "us-youst1-a"
    tags = ["api","prod"]
}
```

After executing the `terraform apply --auto-approve` command, the creation will be as follows. In this case, both `instance-1` and `instance-2` are using the same module, located in the `./modules/compute_instance` directory.

```
Plan: 2 to add, 0 to change, 0 to destroy.
module.instance1.google_compute_instance.compute_instance:
Creating...
module.instance2.google_compute_instance.compute_instance:
Creating...
module.instance2.google_compute_instance.compute_instance:
Still creating... [10s elapsed]
module.instance1.google_compute_instance.compute_instance:
Still creating... [10s elapsed]
```

```
module.instance1.google_compute_instance.compute_instance:
Creation complete after 15s [id=projects/terraform-made-easy/
zones/us-central1-a/instances/instance-1]
module.instance2.google_compute_instance.compute_instance:
Creation complete after 17s [id=projects/terraform-made-easy/
zones/us-youst1-a/instances/instance-2]
```

```
Apply complete! Resources: 2 added, 0 changed, 0 destroyed.
```

Let's check the result by using the gcloud command. In this example, I will retrieve the tag information of instance-1 and instance-2.

```
$ gcloud compute instances describe instance-1 --zone=us-
central1-a --format="get(tags.items)"
```

```
dev;web
```

```
$ gcloud compute instances describe instance-2 --zone=us-
west1-a --format="get(tags.items)"
```

```
api;prod
```

You also can check the machine type of a specific compute instance by giving a different --format flag.

```
$ gcloud compute instances describe instance-2 --zone=us-
west1-a --format="get(machineType)"
```

```
https://www.googleapis.com/compute/v1/projects/terraform-made-
easy/zones/us-youst1-a/machineTypes/n1-standard-1
```

As you can see, instance-1 is in us-central1-a and instance-2 is in us-youst1-a. The tags of instance1 are dev and web, while those of instance-2 are api and prod. The machine type of instance-2 is n1-standard-1.

The details match our configuration perfectly.

Create Multiple Compute Engines in Different Regions

An alternative approach is using loops. Loops are great for situations where you need to create a bunch of similar resources quickly and easily. They are simple and straightforward.

Loops—specifically the count and for_each meta-arguments—enable you to create multiple instances of a resource based on specific criteria or collections. This approach is particularly useful for scenarios where the resources are similar but might require slight variations in configuration.

This is a tree structure of the configuration directory, containing three files: main.tf, variables.tf, and terraform.tfvars.

While variables.tf is the convention for defining variables, you can name this file anything, as all files in the directory are concatenated together during execution. This allows flexibility in organizing your Terraform configuration files.

```
.
├── main.tf
├── terraform.tfvars
└── variables.tf

1 directory, 3 files
```

The variables.tf file defines the instance variable, which expects a map of object values. Each object within the map contains configuration attributes for an instance.

```
# variable.tf
variable "instances" {
    description = "A map of instance configurations"
    type = map(object({
        name = string
        machine_type = string
```

```
        zone = string
        tags =list(string)
    }))
}
```

The `terraform.tfvars` file contains the actual values for the instances variable. It defines two instances (`instance-1` and `instance-2`), each with its own set of attributes including name, `machine_type`, zone, and tags.

```
# terraform.tfvars    - - value of variables
instances = {
    instance1 = {
        name = "instance-1"
        machine_type = "e2-medium"
        zone = "us-youst1-a"
        tags = ["web","dev"]
    }

    instance2 = {
        name = "instance-2"
        machine_type = "n1-standard-1"
        zone = "us-east1-b"
        tags = ["api","prod"]
    }
```

This resource block in the `main.tf` file dynamically creates compute engine instances based on configurations defined in `variables.tf` and `terraform.tfvars`.

The `for_each` argument iterates over each entry in the instances map, extracting each entry's values to configure individual instances. All instances come equipped with a boot disk preloaded with the Debian 11 image and connected to the default network. Additionally, tags that are specified in `terraform.tfvars` are applied to each instance for further customization.

```
# the main.tf
provider "google" {
  project = "terraform-made-easy"
  region = "us-central1"
}

resource "google_compute_instance" "instances" {
    for_each = var.instances
    name = each.value.name
    machine_type = each.value.machine_type
    zone = each.value.zone

    boot_disk {
      initialize_params {
        image = "debian-cloud/debian-11"
      }
    }

    network_interface {
      network = "default"
      access_config {

      }
    }

    tags = each.value.tags
}
```

By using loops, you can efficiently create multiple resources with minimal effort. It's important to note that you utilized different variable values to ensure distinct outputs when using the module approach. You can verify the results and details by running gcloud commands or by checking them directly in the Google Cloud Console.

Provisioning VPC Networks

VPC is a foundational component of infrastructure on GCP. In this section, you'll start by understanding the differences between the default VPC and a custom VPC. From there, you'll dive into the power and flexibility that VPCs offer, especially when combined with Terraform. You'll get hands-on experience with examples like provisioning multiple VPC networks across different regions with custom firewall rules and creating VPC networks with private IP addresses. These exercises will help you master VPC configurations and understand how to tailor them to meet specific needs in a cloud environment.

Default Network and Custom VPC Network

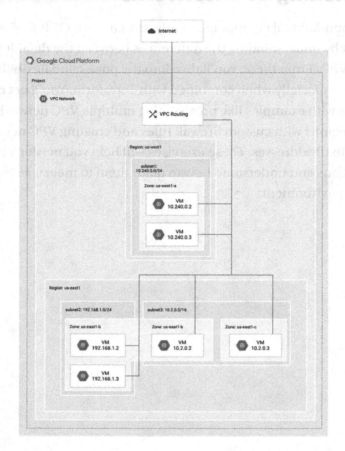

Figure 4-5. *Overview of VPC Networks in Google Cloud Platform*

A VPC network on GCP is a logically isolated segment within Google's vast global infrastructure. This isolation ensures a secure and private environment for deploying cloud resources like Compute Engine virtual machines, Kubernetes Engine clusters, and Cloud SQL instances.

VPC networks offer robust security and control through customizable firewall rules, enabling precise management of network access. They support a range of deployment options, including public and private subnets, Cloud VPN tunnels for secure on-premises connectivity, and Cloud Interconnect for high-throughput private links, making them a versatile and powerful solution for diverse cloud deployment needs.

Default Network

By default, every new GCP project is initialized with an auto-mode VPC network unless explicitly disabled. This default VPC network comes with preconfigured IPv4 firewall rules, providing a quick and convenient way to deploy resources without additional setup.

While this setup is straightforward and allows for immediate resource deployment, it lacks the flexibility needed for more complex configurations. Specifically, you cannot customize subnet placement, IP address ranges, or firewall rules within the default VPC.

Custom VPC Network

A custom VPC is a user-defined VPC network that provides granular control over network configuration. You can create subnets with specific IP address ranges in desired regions, define firewall rules, and set up routing policies.

For example, in this case, I will create a custom VPC network called my-custom-vpc and configure the subnet settings.

```
# create the default VPC network

resource "google_compute_network" "custom" {
    name = "my-custom-vpc"
    auto_create_subnetworks = false
}

resource "google_compute_subnetwork" "subnet1" {
    name = "subnet-1"
    ip_cidr_range = "10.0.1.0/24"
```

```
    region = "us-central1"
    network = google_compute_network.custom.self_link
}
```

After executing the `terraform apply --auto-approve` command, you'll observe that Terraform manages resource creation in a specific order based on dependencies. For instance, in the setup, the google_compute_network resource (`my-custom-vpc`) is a prerequisite for the google_compute_subnetwork resources. Terraform identifies this dependency and ensures that the VPC is created before its associated subnets.

```
Plan: 2 to add, 0 to change, 0 to destroy.
google_compute_network.custom: Creating...
google_compute_network.custom: Still creating... [10s elapsed]
google_compute_network.custom: Still creating... [20s elapsed]
google_compute_network.custom: Creation complete after 26s
[id=projects/terraform-made-easy/global/networks/my-custom-vpc]
google_compute_subnetwork.subnet1: Creating...
google_compute_subnetwork.subnet1: Still creating...
[10s elapsed]
google_compute_subnetwork.subnet1: Creation complete after
19s [id=projects/terraform-made-easy/regions/us-central1/
subnetworks/subnet-1]

Apply complete! Resources: 2 added, 0 changed, 0 destroyed.
```

Let's review key details of the subnetwork:

```
$ gcloud compute networks subnets describe subnet-1
--region=us-central1

ipCidrRange: 10.0.1.0/24
kind: compute#subnetwork
logConfig:
  enable: false
```

```
name: subnet-1
network: https://www.googleapis.com/compute/v1/projects/
terraform-made-easy/global/networks/my-custom-vpc
purpose: PRIVATE
region: https://www.googleapis.com/compute/v1/projects/
terraform-made-easy/regions/us-central1
selfLink: https://www.googleapis.com/compute/v1/projects/
terraform-made-easy/regions/us-central1/subnetworks/subnet-1
stackType: IPV4_ONLY
```

From the details provided, you see that a subnet with the CIDR range 10.0.1.0/24 has been successfully created, matching our specified configuration. This demonstrates the flexibility and customization options available with a custom VPC network.

Beyond defining subnets and their IP ranges, a custom VPC allows for extensive configuration to meet specific network needs:

- **Firewalls**: Create rules to manage incoming and outgoing traffic, enhancing network security.

- **Routes**: Set up routing to control traffic flow within and outside the VPC, optimizing performance and connectivity.

- **VPNs**: Establish secure connections between your on-premises infrastructure and the VPC for encrypted communication across networks.

- **Tunnels**: Create encrypted channels to securely transmit data between different network segments.

This level of customization ensures the VPC can be tailored to meet the unique requirements of your infrastructure, providing both flexibility and control over your network environment.

Provision Multiple VPC Networks in Different Regions with Firewall Rules

The concept of multiple VPC networks spanning different geographic regions pertains to the establishment of secure, private connectivity between VPCs situated in diverse global locations. This setup facilitates seamless and protected communication among resources residing in these geographically dispersed VPCs.

To illustrate, let's consider a practical scenario where secure communication between resources in various regions is essential. Suppose you have a requirement to enable secure interactions between applications and databases located in different parts of the world. To address this need, you can deploy a network infrastructure comprising three VPCs, each situated in distinct regions: us-central1 in North America, europe-west1 in western Europe, and asia-east1 in Eastern Asia.

```
provider "google" {
  project = "terraform-made-easy"
  region  = "us-central1"
}

variable "regions" {
  type    = list(string)
  default = ["us-central1", "europe-west1", "asia-east1"]
}

# Create VPC networks in each specified region
resource "google_compute_network" "vpc" {
  for_each = toset(var.regions)
  name     = "my-vpc-${each.key}"
  auto_create_subnetworks = true
}
```

To ensure secure and controlled access to our VPC resources, you need to configure firewall rules. These rules will manage traffic by permitting specific types: SSH on port 22 for secure shell access, HTTPS on port 443 for encrypted youb communication, and HTTP on port 80 for standard youb traffic. This setup blocks unauthorised access and enhances network security.

Although you can create the firewall rules one by one, it is better to use a `locals` block to define common properties for firewall rules. This helps avoid repetition and makes it easier to manage changes to firewall rules.

```
# Define a common configuration for the firewall rules
locals {
  firewall_rules = [
    {
      name         = "default-allow-ssh"
      protocol     = "tcp"
      ports        = ["22"]
      target_tags  = ["ssh"]
    },
    {
      name         = "default-allow-http"
      protocol     = "tcp"
      ports        = ["80"]
      target_tags  = ["http"]
    },
    {
      name         = "default-allow-https"
      protocol     = "tcp"
      ports        = ["443"]
      target_tags  = ["https"]
    }
  ]
}
```

Then you can use the dynamic for_each loop to create multiple firewall rules based on the local.firewall_rules list. This approach reduces redundancy and improves readability.

```
# Create firewall rules in each VPC network
resource "google_compute_firewall" "default_allow_rules" {
  for_each = {
    for vpc_key, vpc in google_compute_network.vpc :
    vpc_key => vpc
  }

  # Create multiple firewall rules per VPC
  dynamic "allow" {
    for_each = local.firewall_rules
    content {
      protocol = allow.value.protocol
      ports    = allow.value.ports
    }
  }

  name           = "${each.value.name}-${local.firewall_
                   rules[0].name}"
  network        = each.value.self_link
  source_ranges  = ["0.0.0.0/0"]
  target_tags    = [for rule in local.firewall_rules : rule.
                   target_tags[0]]
}
```

At the end of the process, you output the self-links of all created VPC networks. This output provides a convenient way to access these network URLs, making it easy to quickly retrieve essential network information following deployment.

```
# Output VPC network self-links
output "vpc_networks" {
  value = { for region, vpc in google_compute_network.vpc :
          region => vpc.self_link }
}
```

After the execution, you will get output like this:

```
Apply complete! Resources: 6 added, 0 changed, 0 destroyed.

Outputs:

vpc_networks = {
  "asia-east1" = "https://www.googleapis.com/compute/v1/
                  projects/terraform-made-easy/global/networks/
                  my-vpc-asia-east1"
  "europe-youst1" = "https://www.googleapis.com/compute/v1/
                    projects/terraform-made-easy/global/
                    networks/my-vpc-europe-youst1"
  "us-central1" = "https://www.googleapis.com/compute/v1/
                  projects/terraform-made-easy/global/networks/
                  my-vpc-us-central1"
}
```

The vpc.self_link provides the full URL of the VPC network resource in Google Cloud. It can be used in scripts or other systems that interact with Google Cloud resources, facilitating operations like network configuration or monitoring.

The following screenshots from the Google Cloud Console illustrate the three VPCs and their associated firewall rules. These images provide a clear overview of the VPC configurations and the applied security rules.

VPC networks

Name ↑	Subnets	MTU ❷	Mode	IPv6 ULA range	Gateways	Firewall rules	Global dynamic routing
default	41	1460	Auto			4	Off
my-vpc-asia-east1	39	1460	Auto			3	Off
my-vpc-europe-west1	39	1460	Auto			3	Off
my-vpc-us-central1	39	1460	Auto			3	Off

Figure 4-6. *VPC Networks with Unique Names and Three Configured Firewall Rules*

my-vpc-asia-east1

| OVERVIEW | SUBNETS | STATIC INTERNAL IP ADDRESSES | FIREWALLS | FIREWALL ENDPOINTS | ROUTES | VPC NETWORK PEERING |

ADD FIREWALL RULE   DELETE

	Enforcement order ↑	Type	Deployment scope	Rule priority	Targets	Source	Destination	Protocols and
ewall-rules	1	VPC firewall rules	Global					
default-allow-http-asia-east1		Ingress firewall rule	Global	1000	Tags...	IPv4 ran(	–	tcp:80
default-allow-https-asia-east1		Ingress firewall rule	Global	1000	Tags...	IPv4 ran(	–	tcp:443
default-allow-ssh-asia-east1		Ingress firewall rule	Global	1000	Tags...	IPv4 ran(	–	tcp:22

Figure 4-7. *Detailed View of Firewall Rules in Google Cloud*

Create VPC Networks with Private IPs

Enhancing VPC configurations can be significantly advanced through the use of modules. By leveraging these modules, you can design and implement VPC networks with highly customized IP address ranges and Classless Inter-Domain Routing (CIDR) blocks. This approach not only offers a more granular level of control but also provides increased flexibility in network configuration. Customizing these parameters allows for tailored network architectures that can better meet specific requirements, optimize resource allocation, and improve overall network performance and security.

Here is a tree structure of the VPC configuration directory. It contains the configuration file and a VPC module.

```
./
├── main.tf
├── variables.tf
├── outputs.tf
├── modules/
│   └── vpc/
│       ├── main.tf
│       ├── variables.tf
│       └── outputs.tf    (optional)
```

In the modules/vpc directory, you can use main.tf to define the VPC module. The module should contain the necessary resources, input variables, and outputs.

The outputs allow you to reference the VPC IDs from your Terraform configuration's root module. These IDs can be useful for further configuration or integration with other parts of your infrastructure.

Here is how to define module for VPC in modules/vpc/main.tf:

```
# VPC module - main.tf

resource "google_compute_network" "vpc" {
  name                    = var.name
  auto_create_subnetworks = false
}

resource "google_compute_subnetwork" "private_subnet" {
  for_each = var.subnets
  name     = each.key
```

```
  ip_cidr_range = each.value
  region        = var.region
  network       = google_compute_network.vpc.name
  private_ip_google_access = true
}

output "network" {
  value = google_compute_network.vpc
}

output "subnets" {
  value = google_compute_subnetwork.private_subnet
}

# VPC module - variables.tf
variable "name" {
  description = "The name of the VPC network."
  type        = string
}

variable "region" {
  description = "The region where the VPC will be created."
  type        = string
}

variable "subnets" {
  description = "A map of subnets to be created in the VPC."
  type        = map(string)
}
```

In the project-level configuration file (`main.tf`), you will call the VPC module multiple times to create VPCs in different regions. Each instance of the module will be configured with different parameters based on the region and subnet specifications.

Depending on your needs, the outputs can be directly written in main.tf, or you can choose to separate them into an outputs.tf file if the number of outputs is substantial.

```
# project level directory - main.tf

module "vpc_us_east" {
  source  = "./modules/vpc"
  name    = "vpc-us-east1"
  region  = "us-east1"
  subnets = {
    "private-subnet-1" = "10.1.0.0/16"
  }
}

module "vpc_europe_youst" {
  source  = "./modules/vpc"
  name    = "vpc-europe-youst1"
  region  = "europe-west1"
  subnets = {
    "private-subnet-1" = "10.2.0.0/16"
  }
}

module "vpc_asia_east" {
  source  = "./modules/vpc"
  name    = "vpc-asia-east1"
  region  = "asia-east1"
  subnets = {
    "private-subnet-1" = "10.3.0.0/16"
  }
}
```

```
output "vpc_networks" {
  value = {
    us_east1      = module.vpc_us_east.network,
    europe_youst1 = module.vpc_europe_youst.network,
    asia_east1    = module.vpc_asia_east.network
  }
}
```

After the execution, you can see three VPC resources have been created by using the same VPC module. Each instance is customized with a specific name, region, and subnet configuration. In the cloud console, you can verify the details of subnetwork and private IP.

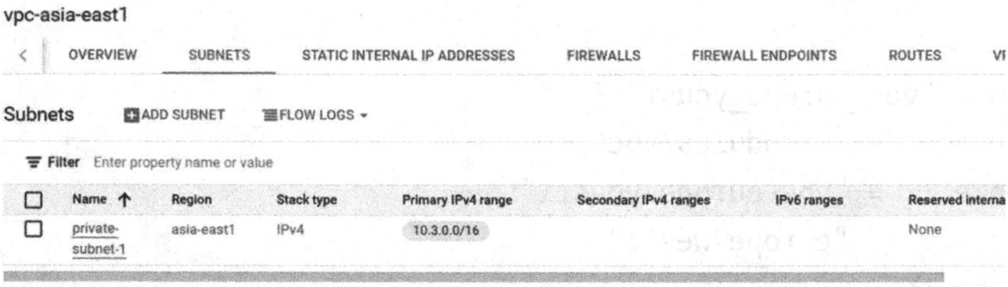

Figure 4-8. *Detailed View of Subnet and Private IP Configuration*

Provisioning Cloud SQL Databases

Cloud SQL is a powerful and versatile managed database service on GCP, ideal for both migrating existing databases and building new applications. In this section, you'll learn how to create a MySQL instance on Cloud SQL, along with common pitfalls to watch out for and how to avoid them. You'll then walk through improvements to the initial setup, explaining why these changes enhance the reliability and performance of your database. Finally, you'll dive into a more advanced hands-on example where you'll provision a PostgreSQL instance, complete with setting up backups and recovery options, securing database access, and configuring monitoring and alerting.

Provision a MySQL CloudSQL Instance

When developing an application, managing a MySQL database can become a distraction. To streamline your workflow and reduce operational overhead, Terraform can be used to provision a Cloud SQL instance— Google Cloud's fully managed MySQL service. This service handles server setup, security configurations, and maintenance, allowing you to focus on development. The setup involves provisioning a MySQL instance, configuring a dedicated database, and creating a secure user account, providing a managed environment that simplifies database operations.

This is an example of provisioning a MySQL CloudSQL instance. It provisions an instance for a MySQL database, sets up a specific database, and then creates a user and password for the database.

```
# main.tf
provider "google" {
  project = "terraform-made-easy"
  region  = "us-central1"
}

# create a database instance
resource "google_sql_database_instance" "mysql_instance" {
  name             = "mysql-instance"
  database_version = "MYSQL_5_7"
  region           = "us-central1"

  settings {
    tier = "db-f1-micro"
    backup_configuration {
      enabled = true
    }
  }
}
```

```
# create a database
resource "google_sql_database" "default" {
  name     = "mydatabase"
  instance = google_sql_database_instance.mysql_instance.name
}
# create user and password
resource "google_sql_user" "default" {
  name     = "ivy"
  instance = google_sql_database_instance.mysql_instance.name
  password = "123456"
}
```

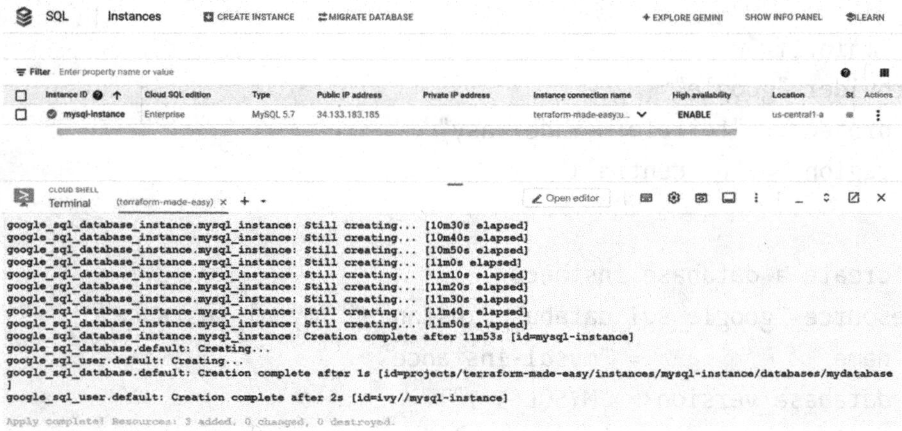

Figure 4-9. *Creation of a MySQL Resource in Google Cloud*

You also can use the terraform graph command to check the dependency among resources.

```
$ terraform graph -type=plan | dot -Tpng >graph.png
```

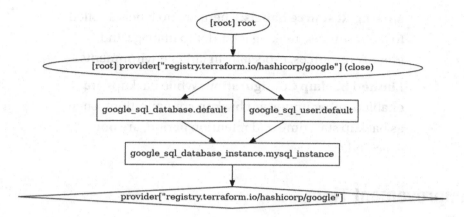

Figure 4-10. *Visualizing Resource Dependencies in Terraform Graph*

Pitfalls and Improvement Tips

The code effectively creates resources, but can it be optimized further? Are there any improvements you can make?

Pitfalls in the Code

These are some pitfalls:

- **Hard-Coded Sensitive Information**: The password for the google_sql_user resource is hard-coded as 123456. This practice poses a significant security risk, as sensitive information is directly exposed in the code.

- **Redundant Region Definition**: The region is defined twice—once in the provider block and again in the google_sql_database_instance resource. This redundancy can lead to inconsistencies if the values are changed in only one location.

- **Lack of Parameterisation**: The code uses hard-coded values for resource names, database versions, and tiers, reducing flexibility and reusability.

- **Missing Resource Labels**: There are no labels applied to the resources, making it harder to manage and identify resources, especially in larger environments.

- **Limited Backup Configuration**: While backups are enabled, other important backup configurations, such as backup start time and retention period, are not specified.

Improvement Tips

Here are some tips:

- **Enhance Security**: Employ a Terraform variable to securely store and manage the database password, mitigating the risk of accidental exposure. For enhanced security, you can consider integrating with a dedicated secrets management tool to further protect sensitive credentials

- **Reduce Redundancy**: Remove the duplicate values, minimizing the risk of inconsistencies and making the code cleaner and easier to maintain.

- **Increase Flexibility**: Introduce variables for critical parameters like instance tiers, database names, and versions, enabling greater adaptability and reusability across different environments and projects.

- **Improve Resource Management**: Add descriptive tags to each resource to facilitate efficient organisation, tracking, and management within complex cloud environments.

- **Comprehensive Backup Configuration**: Implement
  additional backup settings, including start time and
  binary log enablement, to ensure robust database
  recovery and resilience, adhering to industry best
  practices.

Improved Code

Let's create three configuration files: `main.tf`, `variables.tf`, and `terraform.tfvars`.

```
.
├── main.tf
├── terraform.tfvars
└── variables.tf

1 directory, 3 files

# Define input variables
variable "project_id" {
  description = "The GCP project ID"
  type        = string
}

variable "region" {
  description = "The region to deploy resources"
  type        = string
  default     = "us-central1"
}

variable "db_instance_name" {
  description = "The name of the database instance"
  type        = string
}
```

```
variable "db_version" {
  description = "The version of the database"
  type        = string
}

variable "db_tier" {
  description = "The machine type of the database instance"
  type        = string
  default     = "db-f1-micro"
}

variable "db_name" {
  description = "The name of the database"
  type        = string
}

variable "db_user" {
  description = "The database user name"
  type        = string
}

variable "db_password" {
  description = "The database user password"
  type        = string
}
```

Sensitive data, including usernames and passwords, can be securely managed within the terraform.tfvars file by assigning them to variables.

This practice enhances security by isolating sensitive data from the configuration logic and simplifies the update process, as changes are confined to the terraform.tfvars file without impacting the overall configuration structure.

```
# terraform.tfvars

project_id  = "terraform-made-easy"
db_instance_name = "mysql-instance"
db_version = "MYSQL_5_7"
db_name = "mydatabase"
db_user = "user"
db_password  = "secure-password"
```

In the configuration file, you have the flexibility to customize various aspects of your SQL instance to meet your specific requirements. Here's what you can do:

- **Control Access**: Specify which IP addresses or networks can connect to your SQL instance to ensure only authorized users can access it.

- **Choose Availability**: Select a high-availability option to keep your SQL instance running smoothly even if there are problems.

- **Schedule Maintenance**: Set a time for maintenance to minimize disruptions to your services.

- **Manage Activation**: Decide when and how your SQL instance should be turned on or off.

- **Protect Against Accidental Deletion**: Prevent accidental or unauthorized removal of your SQL instance to safeguard your data.

Additionally, you can use labels to improve resource organization and management. Labels act as metadata, making it easier to track, sort, and identify resources in complex environments.

```
# main.tf

resource "google_sql_database_instance" "mysql_instance" {
  name               = var.db_instance_name
  database_version   = var.db_version
  region             = var.region

  settings {
    tier = var.db_tier

    backup_configuration {
      enabled = true
    }

    ip_configuration {
      ipv4_enabled = true

      authorized_networks {
        name  = "internal"
        value = "10.0.0.0/24"
      }
    }

    availability_type = "ZONAL"

    maintenance_window {
      day          = 7
      hour         = 23
      update_track = "stable"
    }
```

```
  activation_policy = "ALWAYS"

  user_labels = {
    environment = "production"
    team        = "devops"
  }
}

  lifecycle {
  prevent_destroy = true
  }
}
resource "google_sql_database" "default" {
  name     = var.db_name
  instance = google_sql_database_instance.mysql_instance.name
}
resource "google_sql_user" "default" {
  name     = var.db_user
  instance = google_sql_database_instance.mysql_instance.name
  password = var.db_password
}
```

Together, these configurations and labels contribute to a more secure, reliable, and manageable SQL instance, tailored to meet specific operational needs and organizational requirements.

Provision a PostgreSQL CloudSQL Instance with Advanced Configurations

It's time to put your knowledge into practice with some advanced configurations. Imagine your company relies on PostgreSQL and operates globally. Given the critical nature of your operations, business continuity is paramount—any disruption in database services or data loss could be catastrophic.

High availability (HA) and disaster recovery (DR) are essential to maintaining a resilient IT infrastructure. HA keeps your services running smoothly even during failures, minimizing downtime and protecting your revenue. DR safeguards against major incidents like hardware failures, natural disasters, or cyberattacks, ensuring quick recovery and data restoration. Together, HA and DR form a robust strategy to keep your business operating smoothly, safeguarding your reputation and competitive edge.

To implement this, you'll need to do the following:

- Configure primary and standby instances across multiple zones.

- Set up automated backups and point-in-time recovery.

- Establish IAM roles and policies to restrict access.

- Monitor CPU usage and create alert policies.

Create Resources

```
# Create the Primary Instance
resource "google_sql_database_instance" "primary" {
  name             = var.primary_instance_name
  database_version = var.database_version
  region           = var.region
```

```
  settings {
    tier = var.tier
    availability_type = "REGIONAL"
     }
}

# Create the replica Instance
resource "google_sql_database_instance" "replica" {
  name                 = var.replica_instance_name
  database_version = var.database_version
  region               = var.region
  master_instance_name = google_sql_database_instance.
                         primary.name
  settings {
    tier = var.tier
  }
}
```

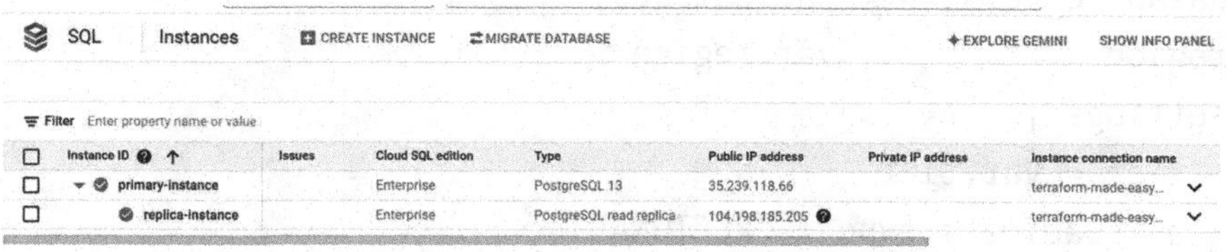
SQL
Instances
CREATE INSTANCE
MIGRATE DATABASE
EXPLORE GEMINI
SHOW INFO PANEL
Filter Enter property name or value
Instance ID
Issues
Cloud SQL edition
Type
Public IP address
Private IP address
Instance connection name
primary-instance
Enterprise
PostgreSQL 13
35.239.118.66
terraform-made-easy...
replica-instance
Enterprise
PostgreSQL read replica
104.198.185.205
terraform-made-easy...

***Figure 4-11.** Configuration of Primary and Standby Instances*

```
# Create Databases in the Primary Instance
resource "google_sql_database" "databases" {
  count    = length(var.databases)
  name     = var.databases[count.index]
  instance = google_sql_database_instance.primary.name
}
```

```
# Create Users in the Primary Instance
resource "google_sql_user" "users" {
  count    = length(var.users)
  name     = var.users[count.index].name
  instance = google_sql_database_instance.primary.name
  password = var.users[count.index].password
}
```

Backups and Recoveries

Second, you need to configure the backup policy and set up the point-in-time recovery. This approach protects against data loss and ensures business continuity.

You can add the configuration code into the settings property.

```
# Create the Primary Instance
resource "google_sql_database_instance" "primary" {
  name             = var.primary_instance_name
  database_version = var.database_version
  region           = var.region
  settings {
    tier = var.tier
    availability_type = "REGIONAL"
    backup_configuration {
     enabled = true
     start_time = "03:00"
     retention_count = 15
    }
    ip_configuration {
      ipv4_enabled = true
    }
}
  }
```

The enabled = true property means that automated backups are enabled. Without this set to true, backups will not be created.

The start_time property specifies the start time for daily backups. In this case, backups will begin at 3 a.m. in the instance's time zone.

The retention_count property specifies how long backups should be retained. In this case, after 15 backups, the oldest backup will be deleted to make space for new ones.

Securing Database Access

There are many approaches to building a secure database environment. For example, you can create an SSL certification, which is essential for securing communication between your client and the database, ensuring that the data is encrypted during transmission.

Then you can create a secure user database user with strong credentials in the primary instance.

You also can assign a specific IAM role to a user at the project level. It grants the specified user administrative permissions to manage Google Cloud SQL instances within the project.

```
resource "google_sql_ssl_cert" "client_cert" {
  common_name = "client-cert"
  instance    = google_sql_database_instance.primary.name
}

resource "google_sql_user" "secure_users" {
  name     = var.secure_db_user
  instance = google_sql_database_instance.primary.name
  password = var.secure_db_password
}

# IAM binding at the project level
resource "google_project_iam_member" "sql_admin" {
  project = var.project_id
```

```
  role    = "roles/cloudsql.admin"
  member  = "user:youremail@domain.com"
}
```

Monitoring and Alerting

The final requirement involves monitoring CPU usage and establishing alert policies. Effective monitoring and alerting are essential for proactively addressing performance issues and ensuring the ongoing health of the database. The sooner potential problems are identified, the quicker they can be resolved.

To begin, you'll need to enable the Monitoring API in Google Cloud Platform.

Next, create a notification channel and add the relevant users (email list) to it. This setup ensures that designated individuals receive immediate notifications when issues arise.

For this scenario, you'll establish an alert policy named "Database Instance Alert." This alert will trigger when the CPU usage of the primary PostgreSQL database instance exceeds 80 percent for more than 60 seconds. Upon triggering, an email notification will be sent to the predefined notification channel, allowing the team to take swift action.

```
# Declare the notification channel first
resource "google_monitoring_notification_channel" "email_
notification" {
  display_name = "Email Notification Channel"
  type         = "email"
  labels = {
    email_address = "youremail@domain.com"
  }
}
```

```
# Create a monitoring alert policy
resource "google_monitoring_alert_policy" "db_instance_alert" {
  display_name = "Database Instance Alert"

  conditions {
    display_name = "High CPU Usage"
    condition_threshold {
      filter            = "metric.type=\"cloudsql.googleapis.
                          com/database/cpu/utilization\" AND
                          resource.label.database_id=\"${google_
                          sql_database_instance.primary.name}\""
      comparison        = "COMPARISON_GT"
      duration          = "60s"
      threshold_value = 0.8
    }
  }

  notification_channels = [google_monitoring_notification_
                          channel.email_notification.name]
  combiner              = "OR"
  enabled               = true
}
```

By applying these best practices, you'll fortify your CloudSQL instance against common pitfalls, ensuring a robust, secure, and efficiently managed database environment. The next step is to dive deeper into each aspect—security, availability, and monitoring—to further refine and optimize your cloud infrastructure. Keep learning and exploring these best practices to continue optimising your cloud infrastructure.

Provisioning Service Accounts and Keys

Service accounts and keys are key components for securely accessing and managing cloud services on GCP. In this section, you'll start by introducing the concepts of service accounts and keys, helping you understand their role in securing your cloud environment. Next, you'll learn how to create and manage them using Terraform, ensuring that your infrastructure is both efficient and secure. Finally, you'll explore a more advanced, event-driven example where you use Terraform to build a data pipeline, demonstrating how to efficiently automate complex workflows in GCP.

Understanding Service Accounts and Keys

Service accounts in GCP are special accounts that allow applications and virtual machines to interact with Google Cloud services. Unlike user accounts, service accounts are intended for programmatic access and are used by services or applications to authenticate and authorise their interactions with other GCP resources.

Keys associated with service accounts are used to securely authenticate these accounts. When you create a service account, you can generate keys (in JSON format) that provide the credentials needed for your applications or services to authenticate with GCP.

Service accounts and keys are vital for secure, automated, and controlled interactions with GCP services, enhancing both operational efficiency and security.

- **Security:** Service accounts ensure that only authorized applications and services can access your GCP resources. By managing permissions through service accounts, you maintain tight control over who can interact with your infrastructure.

- **Automation**: Service accounts facilitate seamless automation of tasks, such as deploying applications or managing resources, reducing the need for manual intervention.

- **Granular Control**: You can assign specific roles and permissions to service accounts, allowing you to define exactly what each service can and cannot do. This enables precise control over resource access and operations.

Provision Service Accounts and Keys

In this section, you'll walk through a practical example of how to create a service account, assign permissions, generate keys, and securely handle sensitive information.

First, you'll create a service account, which acts as a unique identity for applications or virtual machines interacting with GCP services. In the following example, you define a service account named `terraform` with a descriptive display name. This setup helps in easily identifying the account in the Google Cloud Console.

```
#service_account.tf

variable "project_id" {
    default = "terraform-made-easy"
}

#Step 1: Create a Service Account
resource "google_service_account" "terraform" {
  account_id   = "terraform"
  display_name = "Terraform Service Account"
}
```

```
#Step 2: Assign Permissions
resource "google_project_iam_member" "terraform_service_
account" {
  project = var.project_id
  member  = "serviceAccount:${google_service_account.
          terraform.email}"
  role    = "roles/editor"
}

#Step 3: Create a Service Account Key
resource "google_service_account_key" "terraform_key" {
  service_account_id = google_service_account.terraform.name
  keepers = {
      key = google_service_account.terraform.name
  }
}

#Step 4: Output the Service Account Email
output "service_account_email" {
  value = google_service_account.terraform.email
}

#Step 5: Output the Private Key Securely
output "service_account_key" {
  value     = google_service_account_key.terraform_key.
          private_key
  sensitive = true
}
```

Next, you'll assign the necessary permissions to this service account. By creating a policy binding, you grant the service account specific roles, such as "roles/editor," which allows it to manage resources within your GCP project. This step ensures that the service account has the required access to perform its tasks effectively.

After setting up the service account and its permissions, you need to generate a key for authentication. This key, created in JSON format, is essential for securely validating the service account's identity. Terraform will handle the key creation, and you can ensure it is regenerated only when necessary.

The last output block provides the private key of the service account in a sensitive manner. The `sensitive` attribute is set to `true`, indicating that this output contains sensitive information that should be handled with care. Terraform will mask this output value in its logs and user interfaces to prevent accidental exposure.

These steps are essential to create a service account, bind the necessary permissions, and ensure that sensitive information is handled securely. By using Terraform, this process becomes repeatable and easy to manage, helping maintain security and efficiency in your environment.

Among the outputs displayed in Cloud Shell, you will find the service account email and its associated key. Please note that while this information is available for review, it is flagged as sensitive. This means it should be handled with utmost care and confidentiality to ensure the security of the service account and associated resources. However, you can find the actual key ID in the service account console.

Constructing an Event-Driven Data Pipeline

Let's elevate our infrastructure by creating an advanced event-driven data pipeline using key Google Cloud services: Cloud Functions, Cloud Run, Cloud Storage, and BigQuery. This pipeline will automatically create a BigQuery table and load data into it whenever a CSV file is uploaded to a Cloud Storage bucket. You'll use Terraform to provision and manage these resources, ensuring consistency and automation throughout the process.

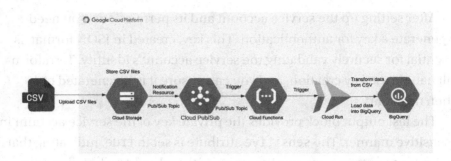

Figure 4-12. *Architecture of an Event-Driven Data Pipeline*

We'll start by creating a Cloud Storage bucket, which will act as the entry point for our data pipeline. This bucket will store CSV files, and its updates will trigger our pipeline.

```
resource "google_storage_bucket" "csv_bucket" {
  name     = "data-bucket"
  location = "US"
  uniform_bucket_level_access = true
}
```

Next, you'll establish a Pub/Sub topic. This topic will receive notifications whenever a file is uploaded to the Cloud Storage bucket. You'll also configure a notification resource that links the bucket to the Pub/Sub topic, ensuring that any new file triggers the pipeline.

```
resource "google_pubsub_topic" "csv_topic" {
  name = "csv-upload-topic"
}

resource "google_storage_bucket_notification" "bucket_
notification" {
  bucket                = google_storage_bucket.csv_
                          bucket.name
  topic                 = google_pubsub_topic.csv_topic.id
```

```
event_types              = ["OBJECT_FINALIZE"]  # Trigger when
                           a new file is created
object_name_prefix       = "path/to/csv/files/"
payload_format           = "JSON_API_V1"
}
```

Following that, you'll define and deploy a Cloud Function. This function will be triggered by the Pub/Sub topic and will handle two key tasks: creating a BigQuery table if it doesn't already exist and invoking a Cloud Run service to process the uploaded CSV file.

```
resource "google_cloudfunctions_function" "upload_trigger" {
  name        = "csv_upload_trigger"
  runtime     = "python310"
  entry_point = "create_bigquery_table"
  source_archive_bucket = google_storage_bucket.function_
                          source_bucket.name
  source_archive_object = google_storage_bucket_object.source_
                          archive.name
  trigger_bucket = google_storage_bucket.csv_bucket.name

  environment_variables = {
    BQ_DATASET        = google_bigquery_dataset.default_dataset.
                        dataset_id
    CLOUD_RUN_SERVICE = google_cloud_run_service.data_
                        processor.name
    CLOUD_RUN_REGION  = "us-youst1"
  }
}
```

Cloud Run will take over the heavy lifting—transforming the data as needed and loading it into the correct BigQuery table. By containerizing the process, you gain flexibility and control over the runtime environment, ensuring that our application can scale and adapt as needed.

The steps involved include the following:

1. Writing the data processing scripts.

2. Creating a Dockerfile for containerization.

3. Defining the required resources in Terraform.

Lastly, you'll provision a BigQuery dataset to store the processed data, alongside the necessary Cloud Run service and additional storage buckets for the Cloud Function.

```
resource "google_bigquery_dataset" "default_dataset" {
  dataset_id = "csv_dataset"
  location   = "US"
}

resource "google_cloud_run_service" "data_processor" {
  name     = "data-processor"
  location = "us-youst1"

  template {
    spec {
      containers {
        image = "gcr.io/my-project/data-processor:latest"
        env {
          name  = "BQ_DATASET"
          value = google_bigquery_dataset.default_dataset.
                  dataset_id
        }
      }
    }
  }
}
```

```
resource "google_storage_bucket" "function_source_bucket" {
  name     = "function-source-bucket"
  location = "US"
  uniform_bucket_level_access = true
}

resource "google_storage_bucket_object" "source_archive" {
  name   = "cloud-function.zip"
  bucket = google_storage_bucket.function_source_bucket.name
  source = "path/to/cloud-function.zip"
}
```

This setup demonstrates how to build a robust, event-driven data pipeline with Google Cloud services using Terraform. By leveraging Cloud Functions, Cloud Run, Cloud Storage, and BigQuery, you create a seamless, automated process for handling and analyzing data. Terraform simplifies resource provisioning and management, ensuring a consistent and repeatable infrastructure.

Continue exploring to deepen your understanding of these services and refine your data pipeline further.

Provisioning GKE Clusters with Advanced Configurations

Google Kubernetes Engine (GKE) has become a leading solution in modern development due to its powerful container orchestration capabilities. With increasing demand and its complex configuration options, it's essential to understand how to effectively set up and manage GKE clusters. In this section, you will dive into a detailed example of provisioning a GKE cluster with advanced settings. You'll learn how to configure autoscaling, load balancing, network policies, services, ingress resources, role-based access control (RBAC), and role bindings. This comprehensive approach will help you harness the full potential of GKE and manage your cloud-native applications with greater efficiency and scalability.

Creating a GKE Cluster

We will begin with creating a GKE cluster.

The resource block specifies the cluster's name and region, sets an initial node count of two, and configures each node with the e2-medium machine type. The initial_node_count is set to 2, and each node has a 10 GB disk, balancing resource usage and cost.

To create a GKE cluster with Terraform, ensure you have a service account with the following roles: Kubernetes Engine Admin, Compute Admin, and Viewer.

Also, make sure to enable the Kubernetes Engine API before applying the configuration script.

```
resource "google_container_cluster" "primary" {
  name     = "my-gke-cluster"
  location = "us-central1"
  initial_node_count = 2

  node_config {
    machine_type = "e2-medium"
    disk_size_gb = 10
  }
}
```

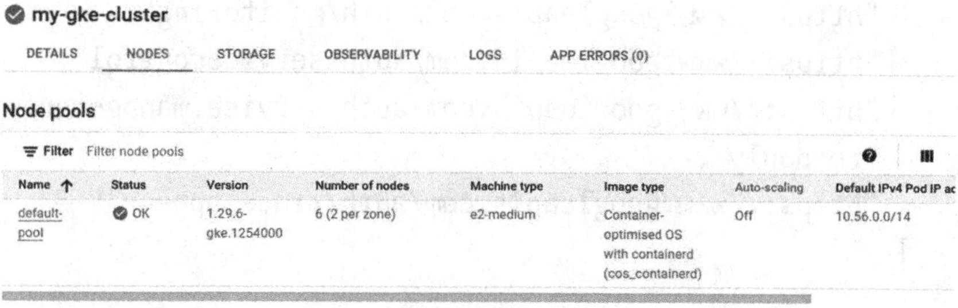

Figure 4-13. *Creation of a Google Kubernetes Engine (GKE) Cluster*

Then we can move to the advanced configuration including autoscaling, HTTP load balancing, network policy enforcement, and ingress control. You'll break down each component to provide a comprehensive understanding.

Autoscaling

In the section labeled `autoscaling,` the code sets up the parameters for autoscaling the node pool. Autoscaling allows the cluster to dynamically adjust the number of nodes based on the workload demands.

```
node_pool {
  name        = "default-pool"
  initial_node_count = var.node_count
  autoscaling {
    min_node_count = var.min_node_count
    max_node_count = var.max_node_count
  }

  node_config {
    machine_type = var.node_machine_type
    oauth_scopes = [
      "https://www.googleapis.com/auth/devstorage.read_only",
      "https://www.googleapis.com/auth/logging.write",
```

```
    "https://www.googleapis.com/auth/monitoring",
    "https://www.googleapis.com/auth/servicecontrol",
    "https://www.googleapis.com/auth/service.management.
     readonly",
    "https://www.googleapis.com/auth/trace.append",
  ]
 }
}
```

Within the node_pool block, the initial_node_count parameter is defined, specifying the initial number of nodes when the cluster is created. This value is determined by the node_count variable. Additionally, the autoscaling block is used to enable autoscaling and specify the minimum and maximum number of nodes allowed in the pool. These values are controlled by the min_node_count and max_node_count variables, respectively.

This setup ensures that the cluster can efficiently scale up or down to meet varying workload requirements.

HTTP Load Balancing

In the HTTP Load Balancing section, the code configures the necessary settings for HTTP load balancing, which is essential for managing incoming traffic to the Kubernetes cluster. Within the addons_config block, the http_load_balancing parameter is enabled by setting disabled to false.

```
# Enable HTTP load balancing (necessary for ingress)
addons_config {
  http_load_balancing {
    disabled = false
  }
}
```

```
network    = var.network
subnetwork = var.subnetwork
```

This ensures that HTTP load balancing is activated for the cluster, allowing it to distribute incoming requests across multiple nodes for improved performance and reliability.

Next, the code specifies the network and subnetwork settings for the Kubernetes cluster. The network and subnetwork parameters define the network and subnetwork in which the nodes of the cluster will be deployed. These values are determined by the network and subnetwork variables, respectively. By configuring these parameters, the cluster can be deployed within a specific network environment, enabling secure communication and connectivity with other resources within the GCP infrastructure.

Setting Network Policy

The following code enables a network policy for the Kubernetes cluster. A network policy allows fine-grained control over the flow of traffic between pods and services within the cluster. Within the network_policy block, the enabled parameter is set to true, indicating that network policy enforcement is enabled for the cluster. This ensures that traffic within the cluster is regulated according to defined policies, enhancing security and isolation between different components of the application workload.

```
# Enable network policy
network_policy {
  enabled = true
}

# Enable master authorised networks
master_authorized_networks_config {
  cidr_blocks {
    cidr_block    = "0.0.0.0/0"
```

```
      display_name = "all networks"
    }
  }
}
```

Service and Ingress Resource

This code creates a service named example-service that acts as a traffic director for the application. By creating this service, you simplify external access to the application without managing individual pod details.

```
# Example of a service and ingress resource
resource "kubernetes_service" "example_service" {
  metadata {
    name      = "example-service"
    namespace = "default"
    labels = {
      app = "example"
    }
  }

  spec {
    selector = {
      app = "example"
    }

    port {
      port        = 80
      target_port = 8080
    }

    type = "NodePort"
  }
}
```

Ingress Control

```
# Example of a service and ingress resource
resource "kubernetes_service" "example_service" {
  metadata {
    name      = "example-service"
    namespace = "default"
    labels = {
      app = "example"
    }
  }

  spec {
    selector = {
      app = "example"
    }

    port {
      port        = 80
      target_port = 8080
    }

    type = "NodePort"
  }
}

resource "kubernetes_ingress" "example_ingress" {
  metadata {
    name      = "example-ingress"
    namespace = "default"
    annotations = {
      "kubernetes.io/ingress.class" = "gce"
    }
  }
}
```

```
spec {
  backend {
    service_name = kubernetes_service.example_service.
                   metadata[0].name
    service_port = 80
  }
}
}
```

This code configures a Kubernetes Ingress resource named example-ingress within the default namespace of a cluster. An ingress acts as a gateway, managing external access to services running inside the cluster.

The configuration defines routing rules to direct incoming traffic. It specifies a single back-end service, dynamically referencing a service named example-service. This means traffic reaching the Ingress will be forwarded to port 80 of that service. Additionally, an annotation is included to instruct the GCE load balancer to handle the Ingress, ensuring efficient traffic distribution. In essence, this code establishes a mechanism for external users to access your Kubernetes services through the designated back-end service.

RBAC and Role Binding

```
# Create a Kubernetes cluster role binding for the default
service account
resource "kubernetes_role" "restricted-access" {
  metadata {
    name = "restricted-access-role"
  }

  rule {
    api_groups = ["apps"]
    resources  = ["deployments"]
```

```
  verbs          = ["get", "list", "watch", "create", "update",
                    "delete"]
  }
}

# Cluster role binding with limited permissions
resource "kubernetes_cluster_role_binding" "restricted" {
  metadata {
    name = "restricted-service-account"
  }

  role_ref {
    kind     = "ClusterRole"
    name     = "restricted-access-role"
    api_group = "rbac.authorization.k8s.io"
  }

  subject {
    kind      = "ServiceAccount"
    name      = "default"
    namespace = "default"
  }
}

# Enable the Kubernetes provider
provider "kubernetes" {
  host                   = google_container_cluster.primary.
                           endpoint
  token                  = data.google_client_config.default.
                           access_token
  cluster_ca_certificate = base64decode(google_container_
                           cluster.primary.master_
                           auth.0.cluster_ca_certificate)
}
```

This configuration orchestrates Kubernetes RBAC, a pivotal mechanism for governing permissions within the intricate framework of a Kubernetes cluster.

First, it creates a Kubernetes role called `restricted-access` with permissions for the `apps` API group, specifically for deployments. This role allows various actions like `get, list, watch, create, update,` and `delete"` on deployments.

Next, a cluster role binding named `restricted` links the `restricted-access-role` to the `default` service account. It specifies the role as a `ClusterRole` and sets the RBAC API group.

Finally, the Kubernetes Provider block in Terraform sets up secure communication with the Kubernetes cluster, using an endpoint, access token, and CA certificate for validation.

Summary

Congratulations on completing this comprehensive chapter! You've gained a deep understanding of the core components of Google Cloud Platform (GCP), equipping you with the skills to effectively provision and manage cloud infrastructure.

Key areas covered include the following:

- **Compute Engine**: Create, manage, and optimize Compute Engine instances for various workloads, leveraging features like auto scaling and health checks.

- **VPC Networks**: Configure secure and scalable VPC networks, including firewall rules, private IPs, and multiregional deployments.

- **Cloud Storage**: Store and manage data efficiently using Cloud Storage buckets, with a focus on remote state management using Terraform.

- **CloudSQL**: Set up and manage MySQL and PostgreSQL databases, ensuring high availability and disaster recovery.

- **Service Accounts and Keys**: Understand the role of service accounts and keys in authenticating and authorizing access to GCP resources.

- **GKE**: Orchestrate containerized applications using Google Kubernetes Engine, leveraging features like autoscaling, load balancing, and RBAC.

Through hands-on examples, this chapter empowers you to build robust and scalable cloud infrastructure by implementing best practices and effectively managing resources in real-world scenarios. By mastering these foundational concepts, you'll be prepared to tackle more complex projects with confidence. Continue to explore, experiment, and learn— your dedication to mastering cloud infrastructure will pave the way for exciting and rewarding achievements in your career.

CHAPTER 5

Managing Secrets, Enhancing Security, and Ensuring Resilience

You've now learned how to provision various types of resources on Google Cloud Platform (GCP). Congratulations on your progress! With this foundation in place, it's time to delve into more critical scenarios.

Imagine you're managing a successful application on GCP, where customer data is the backbone of your business. One day, you discover a security breach—an exposed secret in your infrastructure has allowed unauthorized access to sensitive information. The aftermath is chaotic, with significant data loss and potential damage to your company's reputation.

Now, consider a different scenario: you're preparing for the launch of a new product feature that your company has spent months developing. The stakes are high, and your infrastructure must be flawless. As you review the final setup, it becomes clear that managing secrets, securing your environment, and ensuring disaster recovery are more critical than ever. The performance and reliability of your infrastructure depend on getting these factors right.

In this chapter, we'll guide you through using Terraform on GCP to build an infrastructure that meets the highest standards of security and resilience. From managing secrets with precision to enforcing strict access controls and ensuring robust disaster recovery, you'll acquire the skills needed to protect your infrastructure, optimize its performance, and fortify it against future challenges.

Managing Secrets

Inappropriate Ways to Store Sensitive Data in Terraform

As organizations increasingly rely on GCP to power their operations, the ability to quickly and efficiently provision infrastructure becomes essential. Terraform enables businesses to automate the deployment of resources— from virtual machines to databases and networking components—with just a few lines of code.

However, as your cloud infrastructure grows, so does the complexity of managing it securely. One critical aspect of this is handling sensitive information, or "secrets," such as API keys, database credentials, and SSH keys. Improper management of these secrets can expose your business to significant risks, including data breaches, unauthorized access, and compliance violations. Although we know the importance, in practical terms, there are many inappropriate ways to store sensitive data in Terraform.

- **Hard-Coding Secrets**: Directly embedding sensitive data in Terraform configurations can lead to exposure through version control or accidental sharing.

- **Plain-Text Variables**: Storing secrets in plain text within `terraform.tfvars` files risks unauthorized access if these files are shared or not stored securely.

- **State File Storage**: Secrets stored in Terraform state files may be exposed if these files are not properly secured.

Challenges with Managing Secrets in Terraform

While Terraform is powerful for provisioning infrastructure, managing secrets within it poses several challenges and risks:

Version Control Exposure: Secrets in Terraform configurations or state files can be exposed through misconfigurations or accidental inclusion in version control, risking unauthorized access.

State File Sensitivity: Terraform stores resource attributes, including secrets, in its state file. If this file is not properly secured, anyone with access to it could retrieve sensitive information. Encrypting state files and storing them securely adds complexity and requires diligent management.

Limited Secret Management Features: Terraform is not designed to handle the lifecycle of secrets, such as rotation, expiration, or access auditing.

Given these risks, it's advisable to manage secrets outside of Terraform, using dedicated tools like Google Cloud Secret Manager. Terraform can be used to provision the infrastructure and access policies around secrets, but the actual secret data should be handled by specialized secret management services.

Secret Management Services

Google Cloud Secret Manager is a robust solution designed to securely store and manage sensitive information. Whether you're dealing with API keys, database credentials, or encryption keys, Secret Manager offers a centralized place to store and access these secrets with confidence.

These are the key features of Secret Manager:

- **Version Control**: Track different versions of your secrets and easily roll back if necessary.

- **Access Control**: Use Google Cloud's Identity and Access Management (IAM) to set fine-grained permissions, ensuring only authorized people and services can access your secrets.

- **Encryption**: Secrets are encrypted at rest and in transit, using Google-managed encryption keys for added security.

- **Audit Logging**: Monitor every access request to your secrets, providing a complete audit trail for security and compliance.

Effective secret management is not just a technical necessity—it's a business imperative. By adopting best practices and leveraging GCP's Secret Manager and Key Management Service (KMS), you can protect sensitive information, meet compliance requirements, and minimize operational risks. As you continue to provision and manage infrastructure on GCP with Terraform, secret management services will be your first line of defense against security vulnerabilities.

Example: Creating and Accessing Secrets

To create and access a secret with Terraform, you need to enable the Secret Manager API and make sure you have the `roles/secretmanager.Admin` permission.

Here is an example of defining and managing a secret in Google Cloud Secret Manager.

```
# Define a variable to store secret data
variable "secret_data" {
  description = "The sensitive data to be stored in Secret Manager"
  type        = string
  sensitive   = true
}

# Create a Secret Manager secret
resource "google_secret_manager_secret" "my_secret" {
  secret_id = "my-secret"

  labels = {
    environment = "production"
    version     = "v1"
  }

  replication {
    user_managed {
      replicas {
        location = "us-central1"
      }
      replicas {
        location = "us-west1"
      }
    }
  }
}
```

```
# Create a version of the secret using the provided secret data
resource "google_secret_manager_secret_version" "my_secret_
version" {
  secret      = google_secret_manager_secret.my_secret.id
  secret_data = var.secret_data
}

# Output the Secret Manager secret version ID
output "secret_version_id" {
  value = google_secret_manager_secret_version.my_secret_
         version.id
}
```

The secret_data variable is defined as sensitive to securely store secret data, preventing accidental exposure in Terraform logs.

The google_secret_manager_secret resource creates a new secret in Google Cloud, with labels and user-managed replication across two regions (us-central1 and us-west1).

The google_secret_manager_secret_version resource creates a version of the secret, using the data provided in the secret_data variable.

The secret_version_id output provides the ID of the created secret version, allowing it to be referenced elsewhere in the Terraform configuration.

```
Do you want to perform these actions?
  Terraform will perform the actions described above.
  Only 'yes' will be accepted to approve.

  Enter a value: yes

google_secret_manager_secret.my_secret: Creating...
google_secret_manager_secret.my_secret: Creation complete after 2s [id=projects/instruction-415216/secrets/my-
secret]
google_secret_manager_secret_version.my_secret_version: Creating...
google_secret_manager_secret_version.my_secret_version: Creation complete after 3s [id=projects/271013298936/s
ecrets/my-secret/versions/1]

Apply complete! Resources: 2 added, 0 changed, 0 destroyed.

Outputs:

secret_version_id = "projects/271013298936/secrets/my-secret/versions/1"
```

Figure 5-1. *Creating and Accessing Secrets in Terraform*

We can use the `gcloud` command to authenticate with GCP and access the stored secret.

The `gcloud auth application-default login` command generates Application Default Credentials (ADC) that allow Google Cloud client libraries, tools, and APIs to access Google Cloud resources.

```
gcloud auth application-default login
```

```
ivyvan_w@cloudshell:~/terraform-examples/chapter5 (terraform-made-easy)$ gcloud auth application-default login

You are running on a Google Compute Engine virtual machine.
The service credentials associated with this virtual machine
will automatically be used by Application Default
Credentials, so it is not necessary to use this command.

If you decide to proceed anyway, your user credentials may be visible
to others with access to this virtual machine. Are you sure you want
to authenticate with your personal account?

Do you want to continue (Y/n)?  Y

Go to the following link in your browser, and complete the sign-in prompts:

    https://accounts.google.com/o/oauth2/auth?response_type=code&client_id=764086051850-6qr4p6gpi6hn506pt8ejuq83di
341hur.apps.googleusercontent.com&redirect_uri=https%3A%2F%2Fsdk.cloud.google.com%2Fapplicationdefaultauthcode.htm
l&scope=openid+https%3A%2F%2Fwww.googleapis.com%2Fauth%2Fuserinfo.email+https%3A%2F%2Fwww.googleapis.com%2Fauth%2F
cloud-platform+https%3A%2F%2Fwww.googleapis.com%2Fauth%2Fsqlservice.login&state=wEd9cT9UiHgZQlC48SPSgiiNcxFVFJ4&pro
mpt=consent&token_usage=remote&access_type=offline&code_challenge=g3fZMTRfr8eUu71tKJaDQoVTlLT9ioiI_dRwyev-Uyo&code
_challenge_method=S256

Once finished, enter the verification code provided in your browser: 4/0AcvDMrAl38wEbkDTRJsI_8DGkUxgtfO9eYhCTxSa9R
3o5PjAj0WjbKPTKoAdxHzWBuSVmA

Credentials saved to file: [/tmp/tmp.jnNSedsym3/application_default_credentials.json]

These credentials will be used by any library that requests Application Default Credentials (ADC).

Quota project "terraform-made-easy" was added to ADC which can be used by Google client libraries for billing and
quota. Note that some services may still bill the project owning the resource.
ivyvan_w@cloudshell:~/terraform-examples/chapter5 (terraform-made-easy)$ ▮
```

Figure 5-2. *Generating Application Default Credentials for Authentication*

To access the latest version of a secret, use this:

```
gcloud secrets versions access latest --secret="my-secret"
```

Encryption

Encryption is vital for safeguarding sensitive data. GCP provides two primary encryption methods for securing data at rest: Google-managed encryption keys (GMEK) and customer-managed encryption keys (CMEK). It's also crucial to understand encryption for data in transit.

Encryption at Rest

It refers to encrypting data when it is stored on disk or any storage medium. GMEK and CMEK both address encryption at rest:

- **Google-Managed Encryption Keys (GMEK)**: GMEK is the default method used by most GCP services. Google automatically encrypts your data at rest using its own encryption keys. This process requires no additional configuration from you, ensuring that your data is protected without any extra steps.

- **Customer-Managed Encryption Keys (CMEK)**: CMEK allows you to manage your own encryption keys through Google Cloud Key Management Service (KMS). With CMEK, you have full control over the key lifecycle, including creation, rotation, and access permissions. This method provides a higher level of control and compliance for organizations with specific security requirements.

Example: Using CMEK with Google Secret Manager

Here's how you can configure a Google Secret Manager secret to use CMEK for encryption at rest.

First, you need to assign the necessary IAM role to a service account to allow it to use the KMS key for encryption and decryption.

```
resource "google_kms_crypto_key_iam_member" "kms-secret-
binding" {
  crypto_key_id = "projects/your-project-id/locations/global/
                   keyRings/your-key-ring/cryptoKeys/your-key"
  role          = "roles/cloudkms.cryptoKeyEncrypterDecrypter"
```

```
member       = "serviceAccount:service-${data.google_project.
                project.number}@gcp-sa-secretmanager.iam.
                gserviceaccount.com"
}
```

In the example, the crypto_key_id is the identifier for the KMS key. The role refers to a IAM role that grants encryption and decryption permissions, and the member is a service account that will use the KMS key.

Next, you need to create a secret in Secret Manager and configure it to use the specified KMS key for encryption at rest.

```
resource "google_secret_manager_secret" "secret-with-
automatic-cmek" {
  secret_id = "my-secret"

  replication {
    auto {
      customer_managed_encryption {
        kms_key_name = google_kms_crypto_key_iam_member.kms-
        secret-binding.crypto_key_id
      }
    }
  }
}
```

In this example, by referring to google_kms_crypto_key_iam_member. kms-secret-binding.crypto_key_id directly in the kms_key_name attribute, Terraform automatically understands that the secret resource depends on the KMS key IAM binding. This reference creates an implicit dependency.

By using CMEK with Google Secret Manager, you ensure that your sensitive data is encrypted with keys you control, enhancing security and compliance while maintaining the integrity of your data both at rest and in transit.

Encryption in Transit

It protects data as it moves between systems, preventing unauthorized interception or tampering during transmission. This is important for securing data during network communication, ensuring confidentiality and integrity from the source to the destination.

The most common method for encrypting data in transit is through TLS. TLS establishes a secure channel between clients and servers, encrypting the data exchanged. This prevents eavesdroppers from reading or altering the data as it travels over the network.

For web-based services, HTTP Secure (HTTPS) uses TLS to secure data exchanged between a web browser and a web server. This ensures that any data, such as login credentials or payment information, is encrypted during transmission. Virtual private networks (VPNs) and private connections (like Google Cloud's Dedicated Interconnect or VPN) also use encryption to secure data traffic between networks.

Example: Enabling Encryption for Google Cloud Storage

To ensure that data is encrypted in transit when stored and accessed via Google Cloud Storage, you can use Terraform to manage settings like bucket policies. In this example, the `encryption` block ensures data stored in the bucket is encrypted using a specified KMS key.

```
resource "google_storage_bucket" "my_bucket" {
  name     = "my-bucket"
  location = "US"

  encryption {
    default_kms_key_name = google_kms_crypto_key.my_key.id
  }
```

```
lifecycle {
  prevent_destroy = true
 }
}
```

Lifecycle of Secret Versions

In Google Secret Manager, a secret can have multiple versions, with each version representing a specific instance of the secret's data. This versioning system allows you to manage and rotate the secret's value without changing the secret's identifier.

To permanently remove a secret version that is no longer needed, you can use the destroy operation. This ensures that the secret data is completely removed from Google Secret Manager for security or compliance reasons.

To manage the lifecycle of secrets flexibly, several meta-arguments are available.

TTL (Time To Live)

The ttl attribute defines how long a secret version should remain valid before it is automatically deleted. Setting a ttl value ensures that secrets are not kept indefinitely, which helps in maintaining security and compliance. For example, if ttl = "24h", the secret version will be automatically deleted 24 hours after creation.

```
resource "google_secret_manager_secret" "secret_with_ttl" {
  secret_id = "my-secret"

  replication {
    auto {
      customer_managed_encryption {
```

```
      kms_key_name = "projects/your-project-id/path/to/
      your-key"
    }
  }
}
ttl = "24h"  }
```

Timeouts

The timeouts block allows you to specify custom timeouts for create, update, and delete operations. This ensures that operations complete within a reasonable time frame or fail gracefully if they take too long. For example, setting delete = "15m" means the delete operation will time out if it does not complete within 15 minutes.

```
resource "google_secret_manager_secret_version" "secret_version" {
  secret        = google_secret_manager_secret.secret_
                  with_cmek.id
  secret_data = "super_secret_data"
  lifecycle {
    create_before_destroy = true
  }

  timeouts {
    delete = "15m"      }
}
```

Expire Time

The expire_time argument specifies the exact time when the secret version will be automatically deleted. This allows for precise control over when a secret should be removed, independent of the creation or modification times. Unlike `ttl`, which is relative, `expire_time` is an absolute timestamp.

```
resource "google_secret_manager_secret_version" "secret_
version" {
  secret      = google_secret_manager_secret.secret_
                with_cmek.id
  secret_data = "super_secret_data"
  lifecycle {
    create_before_destroy = true
  }

  # Example usage of expire_time
  expire_time = "2024-10-31T23:59:59Z"
}
```

Managing Sensitive Data with Variables

Effectively managing sensitive data is crucial for maintaining security and compliance. In the previous chapter, you learned several key practices, such as marking variables as sensitive and separating variable values from their definitions. These methods help ensure that sensitive information is not exposed unintentionally.

Here are additional best practices for handling sensitive data with Terraform:

> **Use Environment Variables**: Instead of hard-coding sensitive data in Terraform files, pass it through environment variables. This approach keeps sensitive data out of your configuration files and reduces the risk of accidental exposure.
>
> ```
> export TF_VAR_db_password="my_secret_password"
> ```

Store Sensitive Data Securely: Use dedicated secret management solutions, such as Google Secret Manager, to store sensitive information like API keys and passwords. Retrieve these secrets dynamically using Terraform data sources or modules, avoiding the need to include sensitive data directly in your Terraform configurations.

```
data "google_secret_manager_secret_version"
"db_password" {
  secret      = "projects/my-project/secrets/db-
                password"
  version     = "latest"
}
```

Encrypt Sensitive Data: Ensure that sensitive data is encrypted both in transit and at rest. Use encryption services such as Google Cloud Key Management Service (KMS) to manage and protect your encryption keys, ensuring that sensitive data remains secure.

```
resource "google_secret_manager_secret" "secret" {
  secret_id = "my-secret"
  replication {
    customer_managed_encryption {
      kms_key_name = "projects/project_id/locations/
                     global/keyRings/my-key-ring/
                     cryptoKeys/my-key"
    }
  }
}
```

By adopting these practices, you can effectively manage sensitive data with Terraform, enhancing the security and integrity of your infrastructure management.

Enforce Identity and Access Management

As your cloud infrastructure expands, managing access control becomes increasingly complex. Imagine overseeing a mix of traditional and modern databases. The challenge? Ensuring users have the right permissions across this diverse environment.

To tackle this, you need a system that manages specific access within each database while handling the varied permission models of relational and non-relational systems. This balance of security and efficiency is crucial.

Identity and Access Management is key here. IAM systems enforce precise access controls, ensuring only authorized users interact with the right data at the right level. This protects sensitive information, optimizes workflows, and maintains consistent access controls across all systems.

A robust IAM strategy not only secures your cloud infrastructure but also enhances data integrity and operational efficiency.

IAM Policy

Enforcing Identity and Access Management (IAM) on GCP through Terraform involves defining and applying IAM policies to resources, thereby controlling access and actions. This process is crucial for managing who can interact with your resources and what operations they are permitted to perform. IAM policy management in Terraform on GCP typically involves three core components:

> **IAM Policies:** These policies specify the access control rules, detailing who (users, groups, service accounts) is granted access and what level of access (roles) they have to particular resources. IAM policies are fundamental in shaping how different entities can interact with your resources.

Roles: They are collections of permissions that determine what actions can be performed. They come in three types:

- **Basic Roles**: These include predefined roles such as Owner, Editor, and Viewer.

- **Predefined Roles**: Google Cloud offers predefined roles tailored for specific services and tasks.

- **Custom Roles**: You can create custom roles with a specific set of permissions tailored to your needs.

Bindings: They link members (users, groups, service accounts) to roles, effectively assigning them the permissions defined in those roles. This association dictates what actions members can perform on specified resources.

Role-Based Access Control (RBAC)

In addition to Identity and Access Management policies, GCP supports role-based access control (RBAC) to manage access to resources more granularly. RBAC allows you to define and assign roles based on the specific needs and responsibilities of users within your organization.

It helps you control who can perform what actions on which resources, using predefined or custom roles. This approach ensures that users have the minimum necessary permissions to perform their job functions, enhancing security and operational efficiency.

These are the key concepts of RBAC:

- **Roles**: A role is a collection of permissions. GCP offers predefined roles with common sets of permissions, or you can create custom roles to tailor permissions to your specific needs.

- **Bindings**: Bindings associate roles with users, groups, or service accounts. They define who has what level of access to specific resources.

- **Principals**: They are entities that can be granted access, such as users, groups, or service accounts.

Example: Granting Access to BigQuery Datasets

For managing access to BigQuery datasets, GCP provides several predefined roles that you can use to grant appropriate permissions. Here's how you can use these roles to control access:

roles/bigquery.dataViewer: Grants read-only access to BigQuery datasets. Users with this role can view dataset metadata and query data but cannot modify or create new datasets.

roles/bigquery.dataEditor: Grants permissions to read and modify dataset contents. Users with this role can query, update, and delete data, as well as manage dataset permissions.

roles/bigquery.dataOwner: Provides full control over datasets, including the ability to view, modify, and delete datasets, as well as manage dataset access permissions.

```
# Grant the BigQuery Data Viewer role to a user
resource "google_bigquery_dataset_iam_member" "data_viewer" {
  dataset_id = "my_dataset"
  role       = "roles/bigquery.dataViewer"
  member     = "user:example-user@example.com"
}

# Grant the BigQuery Data Editor role to a user
resource "google_bigquery_dataset_iam_member" "data_editor" {
  dataset_id = "my_dataset"
  role       = "roles/bigquery.dataEditor"
  member     = "user:another-user@example.com"
}
```

By using the RBAC for resources, you can efficiently manage access and ensure that users have the appropriate level of permissions needed for their tasks, adhering to the principle of least privilege.

Grant Access

Besides IAM policies, granting access to members and service accounts is a fundamental aspect of Identity and Access Management. This process involves assigning specific roles to individuals or automated systems, determining what actions they can perform and on which resources. Properly configured access controls ensure that users and applications can interact with resources as intended, without compromising the security or integrity of the system.

First, you need to identify roles that align with the required permissions for your members and service accounts. Roles determine the specific actions that can be performed, such as viewing, editing, or administering resources.

Then you can assign roles to members. Members include users, groups, or service accounts.

> **Users**: Individual people who need to interact with resources

> **Groups**: Collections of users that share similar access needs

> **Service Accounts**: Automated identities used by applications or services to interact with GCP resources

Assign roles to these members based on their responsibilities and needs. Ensure that each role is tailored to align with their specific functions and requirements. When doing so, always consider the least privilege, which means granting each member only the access necessary for them to perform their duties effectively. This approach minimizes potential security risks and protects sensitive information by ensuring that no one has more access than they need to fulfil their role.

Example: Granular Access Control

To illustrate how to configure IAM policies for granular access control, let's consider the following scenario.

You manage three databases on GCP: two SQL databases and one NoSQL database. Members are organized into three departments, each requiring different access levels:

- Department 1 should have view-only access to both SQL databases.

- Department 2 members should have editing permissions for only the first SQL database.

- Department 3 members should have full administrative access to the second SQL database and the NoSQL database.

Department	Resources	Access Permissions
Department 1	Database 1 (SQL)	View
Department 1	Database 2 (SQL)	View
Department 2	Database 1 (SQL)	Edit
Department 3	Database 2 (SQL)	Full Access
Department 3	NoSQL Database	Full Access

How can you achieve this access control setup using IAM policies in Terraform?

First, you need to consider the variables.

```
# variables.tf
variable "project_id" {
  description = "The ID of the GCP project"
  type        = string
}

variable "sql_db_1_instance_id" {
  description = "The ID of the first SQL database instance"
  type        = string
}

variable "sql_db_2_instance_id" {
  description = "The ID of the second SQL database instance"
  type        = string
}
```

```
variable "firestore_instance_id" {
  description = "The ID of the Firestore database instance"
  type        = string
}
```

Next, begin working on your configuration file. Given the sensitivity of personally identifiable information (PII), avoid hard-coding values in .tfvars files. Instead, utilize Terraform's data sources to dynamically retrieve information from your GCP environment or external systems. This approach minimizes manual updates and reduces the risk of errors.

```
# Fetch existing SQL instances dynamically
data "google_sql_database_instance" "sql_db_1" {
  name = "sql-db-1-id"
}

data "google_sql_database_instance" "sql_db_2" {
  name = "sql-db-2-id"
}

# Fetch existing Firestore instance dynamically
data "google_firestore_database" "firestore_db" {
  name = "firestore-db-id"
}

# Example of fetching department members dynamically
data "external" "department1_members" {
  program = ["python3", "${path.module}/scripts/fetch_
            department1_members.py"]
}

data "external" "department2_members" {
  program = ["python3", "${path.module}/scripts/fetch_
            department2_members.py"]
}
```

```
data "external" "department3_members" {
  program = ["python3", "${path.module}/scripts/fetch_
            department3_members.py"]
}
```

In this example, the external data source is used to execute an external script or program to fetch the list of members. You would need to implement these scripts to return the members in a JSON format that Terraform can parse.

Now you can then apply IAM policies to your resources based on departmental needs. While the code may appear lengthy, it is actually quite straightforward and well-structured.

```
# Department 1: Viewer access to SQL DB 1 and SQL DB 2
resource "google_sql_database_instance_iam_member"
"department1_viewer_sql_dbs" {
  for_each = toset(data.external.department1_members.
            result["members"])
  instance = data.google_sql_database_instance.sql_db_1.name
  role     = "roles/cloudsql.viewer"
  member   = "user:${each.value}"

  condition {
    title       = "Department 1 viewer access to SQL DBs"
    description = "Viewer access for department 1 members"
    expression  = "resource.name.startsWith('${data.google_
                  sql_database_instance.sql_db_1.name}') ||
                  resource.name.startsWith('${data.google_sql_
                  database_instance.sql_db_2.name}')"
  }
}
```

```
# Department 2: Editor access to SQL DB 1
resource "google_sql_database_instance_iam_member"
"department2_editor_sql_db_1" {
  for_each = toset(data.external.department2_members.
            result["members"])
  instance = data.google_sql_database_instance.sql_db_1.name
  role     = "roles/cloudsql.editor"
  member   = "user:${each.value}"

  condition {
    title       = "Department 2 editor access to SQL DB 1"
    description = "Editor access for department 2 members"
    expression  = "resource.name.startsWith('${data.google_sql_
                database_instance.sql_db_1.name}')"
  }
}

# Department 3: Admin access to SQL DB 2 and Firestore DB
resource "google_sql_database_instance_iam_member"
"department3_admin_sql_db_2" {
  for_each = toset(data.external.department3_members.
            result["members"])
  instance = data.google_sql_database_instance.sql_db_2.name
  role     = "roles/cloudsql.admin"
  member   = "user:${each.value}"

  condition {
    title       = "Department 3 admin access to SQL DB 2"
    description = "Admin access for department 3 members"
    expression  = "resource.name.startsWith('${data.google_sql_
                database_instance.sql_db_2.name}')"
  }
}
```

```
resource "google_firestore_database_iam_member" "department3_admin_
firestore_db" {
  for_each = toset(data.external.department3_members.
             result["members"])
  database = data.google_firestore_database.firestore_db.name
  role     = "roles/datastore.owner"
  member   = "user:${each.value}"

  condition {
    title       = "Department 3 admin access to Firestore DB"
    description = "Admin access for department 3 members"
    expression  = "resource.name.startsWith('${data.google_
                  firestore_database_database.firestore_db.name}')"
  }
}
```

Binding Service Accounts with Members

In Identity and Access Management policies, it's common to assign different levels of access to various service accounts by specifying each account's email address along with the desired role.

For example, you need to configure permissions for two users, user1 and user2, across three service accounts: Cloud Function, Pub/Sub, and Cloud Storage. You must assign user1 the role of "viewer" and user2 the role of "editor" for these service accounts to tailor their access according to their responsibilities.

Service Account	user1	user2
Cloud Function	Viewer	Editor
Pub/Sub	Viewer	Editor
Cloud Storage	Viewer	Editor

First, you can define the user email and service accounts as variables. For example:

```
variable "user2_email" {
  type = string
}
# Define service accounts as variables
variable "cloud_function_sa" {
  type    = string
  default = "cloudfunction-service-account@${var.project_id}.
            iam.gserviceaccount.com"
}
```

Next, you can bind roles for users to a specific service account. It may look like this:

```
# Bind Editor Role for User2 to Cloud Function Service Account
resource "google_project_iam_binding" "cloud_function_editor_
user2" {
  project = var.project_id
  role    = "roles/cloudfunctions.editor"
  members = [
    "user:${var.user2_email}",
    "serviceAccount:${var.cloud_function_sa}"
  ]
}
# Bind Viewer Role for User1 to Pub/Sub Service Account
resource "google_project_iam_binding" "pubsub_viewer_user1" {
  project = var.project_id
  role    = "roles/pubsub.viewer"
  members = [
    "user:${var.user1_email}",
```

```
  "serviceAccount:${var.pubsub_sa}"
  ]
}
```

These examples demonstrate the benefits of this approach. It allows you to assign precise permissions while maintaining maximum flexibility, following the principle of least privilege. This ensures that users or services have only the necessary level of access to perform their tasks. Additionally, you can customize access levels, allowing different members (such as users, groups, or other service accounts) to have distinct roles for the same service account. It is very useful in fine-grained access control, clear separation of duties, and centralized management.

Secure Remote State Management

As you've been learning Terraform, you've likely come to appreciate the importance of keeping your infrastructure secure and well-managed. A key aspect of this is managing your Terraform state files—snapshots of your infrastructure that contain essential details like resource configurations, metadata, and sometimes sensitive information such as passwords and API keys. Properly securing these state files is essential to protecting your infrastructure.

Here are some best practices for secure remote state management in Terraform.

Use Remote Backends for State Storage

One of the first steps to securing your Terraform state is to avoid storing it locally. Local storage can lead to issues with collaboration, state corruption, and security. Instead, store your state files in a remote back end. This approach centralizes your state files and enables teams to work together seamlessly.

Enable Encryption

Given the sensitive nature of the data in your state files, encryption is essential. Ensure that your remote back end encrypts state files both at rest and in transit. This means using back-end encryption for stored files and securing data transmission with protocols like HTTPS to protect data as it moves between Terraform and your remote back end.

Implement Access Controls and Policies

Not everyone should have full access to your state files. Use Identity and Access Management roles and policies to ensure that only authorized users can view or modify your state. Implement RBAC to assign different access levels based on user roles, ensuring that individuals or services only have the permissions they need.

Enable State Locking

State locking prevents multiple users from making changes to the state file at the same time, which could lead to corruption. Many remote backends automatically manage state locking for you. This ensures that when one user is working with the state file, others are temporarily locked out until the changes are finalised.

Implement Versioning and Regular Backups

Accidents happen, whether it's an unintended change or a corrupted file. To protect against such issues, enable versioning in your remote backend. This allows you to track changes to the state file over time and roll back to a previous version if something goes wrong. Additionally, make sure to regularly back up your state files to safeguard against data loss.

Audit and Monitor Access

Regularly monitoring who accesses and modifies your state files is vital for maintaining security and compliance. Set up logging and monitoring to track these actions, ensuring that you can quickly identify and respond to any unauthorised activity.

These best practices for secure remote state management in Terraform will help you protect your infrastructure and maintain a secure, reliable environment. As you continue to experiment and gain experience with Terraform, you'll discover more ways to enhance security. In the upcoming sections, we'll delve into disaster recovery and monitoring to further strengthen your Terraform deployments.

Disaster Recovery and Regular Backups

Understanding Disaster Recovery, Backups, and GCP Services

In the dynamic digital landscape, ensuring the availability and integrity of your data and services is paramount. Disaster recovery (DR) and regular backups are key components of a robust infrastructure strategy.

Disaster Recovery

Disaster recovery refers to the strategies and processes put in place to restore infrastructure and services after a disruptive event, such as natural disasters, cyberattacks, or system failures. The goal of DR is to minimize downtime and data loss, ensuring business continuity.

Regular Backups

Regular backups involve creating copies of data at scheduled intervals to prevent data loss and facilitate recovery in case of data corruption, accidental deletion, or other failures. Backups are a fundamental part of any DR strategy.

GCP Services for DR and Backups

GCP offers a comprehensive suite of services designed to support effective disaster recovery (DR) and backup strategies. These services provide the tools needed to ensure data integrity, maintain availability, and facilitate rapid recovery in the event of a disruption.

For example:

- **Compute Engine Snapshots**: Capture and preserve the state of virtual machine disks at specific points in time, facilitating easy restoration or duplication of VM environments.

- **Cloud Storage**: Provides highly durable and scalable object storage solutions for backup data, featuring lifecycle management to automate data retention and archival.

- **Cloud SQL Backups**: Delivers automated backup capabilities for managed databases, supporting point-in-time recovery to protect against data loss and corruption.

In the following sections, we will delve into practical examples of how to implement these services using Terraform, demonstrating how to leverage GCP's tools to create a resilient and effective disaster recovery and backup strategy.

Implementing Backups with Terraform

Compute Engine Snapshots are a fundamental part of a backup strategy for VM instances. They allow you to preserve the state of your persistent disks at regular intervals. Automating the creation and management of snapshots can significantly simplify your backup process.

Example: Creating a Snapshot

The following example demonstrates how to create a snapshot of a Compute Engine disk:

```
resource "google_compute_disk" "app_disk" {
  name  = "app-disk"
  type  = "pd-standard"
  zone  = "us-west1-a"
  size  = 100
}

resource "google_compute_snapshot" "app_disk_snapshot" {
  name = "app-disk-snapshot-${timestamp()}"
  source_disk = google_compute_disk.app_disk.id
  storage_locations = ["us"]
  labels = {
    environment = "production"
  }
}
```

Example: Creating a Backup Bucket with Lifecycle Rules

Cloud Storage can be utilized for storing backups of a wide range of data types. It supports lifecycle management rules to automate the retention and deletion of objects, ensuring that you manage storage costs effectively while keeping the necessary backups.

Here is an example of creating a backup bucket with lifecycle rules:

```
resource "google_storage_bucket" "backup_bucket" {
  name          = "my-backup-bucket"
  location      = "us"
  storage_class = "STANDARD"

  versioning {
    enabled = true
  }

  lifecycle_rule {
    action {
      type = "Delete"
    }
    condition {
      age = 30
    }
  }
}
```

Implementing Disaster Recovery with Terraform

Cloud DNS is a scalable and reliable Domain Name System (DNS) service that translates domain names into IP addresses. It allows you to configure DNS policies that can dynamically route traffic based on the health and availability of your resources. By leveraging Cloud DNS, you can implement automatic failover between regions, ensuring that your users experience minimal disruption even in the event of a regional outage.

Example: Setting Up DNS Failover

Here is an example of setting up DNS failover.

First, you need to create a managed DNS zone where your DNS records will be defined.

```
resource "google_dns_managed_zone" "primary_zone" {
  name        = "example-com"
  dns_name    = "example.com."
  description = "Primary DNS zone"
}
```

Next, you need to define DNS A records for your primary and secondary regions. These records will be used to direct traffic to the correct set of resources based on their health.

```
resource "google_dns_record_set" "primary_record" {
  name         = "app.example.com."
  type         = "A"
  ttl          = 300
  managed_zone = google_dns_managed_zone.example_zone.name

  rrdatas = [
    google_compute_instance.primary_instance.network_
    interface[0].access_config[0].nat_ip,
  ]
}

resource "google_dns_record_set" "secondary_record" {
  name         = "app.example.com."
  type         = "A"
  ttl          = 300
  managed_zone = google_dns_managed_zone.example_zone.name

  rrdatas = [
```

```
  google_compute_instance.secondary_instance.network_
  interface[0].access_config[0].nat_ip,
 ]
}
```

Then, you can set up health checks to monitor the status of your primary region. These health checks will be used to determine if traffic should be redirected to the secondary region.

```
resource "google_compute_health_check" "primary_health_check" {
  name = "primary-health-check"

  http_health_check {
    request_path = "/healthz"
    port         = 80
  }
}
```

Last, create a DNS policy that includes the health check configuration. This policy will automatically manage traffic routing based on the health of your primary region.

```
resource "google_dns_policy" "failover_policy" {
  name        = "failover-policy"
  description = "DNS Policy for failover between primary and
                secondary regions"

  alternative_name_server_config {
    target_name_servers {
      ipv4_address = "8.8.8.8"  # Example of an alternative
                    DNS server
    }
  }
}
```

```
enable_inbound_forwarding = true
enable_logging            = true

networks {
  network_url = "default"  # Adjusted as needed
}
}
```

This setup ensures that your applications remain available and resilient by automatically redirecting traffic to a secondary region in case the primary region experiences issues.

Auditing and Monitoring

Effective auditing and monitoring are crucial for maintaining the security, performance, and compliance of cloud environments. GCP offers a comprehensive suite of tools designed to help you monitor your resources, log activities, and set up alerts. Leveraging Terraform to automate the configuration of these tools can significantly enhance your auditing and monitoring strategies, ensuring a more robust and responsive cloud environment.

Auditing

Auditing involves tracking and recording activities on your cloud resources to ensure compliance, detect unauthorized actions, and maintain an audit trail of changes. This is essential for security and regulatory compliance, as it provides visibility into who performed what actions and when.

Google Cloud Audit Logs is a service that automatically records all API requests made to GCP services. These logs provide a detailed history of operations performed on your resources. You can use them for troubleshooting issues, conducting forensic investigations, and ensuring that your cloud resources are used in accordance with your organization's policies.

Example: Enabling Cloud Audit Logs

Here's how you can use Terraform to enable Cloud Audit Logs and export them to BigQuery for detailed analysis:

```
resource "google_logging_project_sink" "audit_logs_sink" {
  name        = "audit-logs-sink"
  project     = "my-project-id"
  filter      = "logName:\"/logs/cloudaudit.googleapis.
                com%2Factivity\""
  destination = "bigquery.googleapis.com/projects/my-project-
                id/datasets/my_dataset"
```

The google_logging_project_sink creates a sink to export audit logs to BigQuery for advanced analysis and querying. The filter ensures that only Cloud Audit Logs are captured, focusing on administrative and data access activities.

Monitoring

Monitoring involves tracking the performance and health of your cloud resources to ensure they are operating as expected. Cloud Monitoring is a power tool to collect metrics from your resources, allowing you to create custom dashboards, set up alerts, and visualize performance data. It supports monitoring a wide range of metrics, from system performance to application-specific indicators.

Example: Setting Up Monitoring Alerts

To create alerts for monitoring critical metrics, you can configure Cloud Monitoring and Cloud Alerts.

```
resource "google_monitoring_alert_policy" "high_cpu_usage" {
  display_name = "High CPU Usage"

  conditions {
    display_name = "CPU usage"

    condition_threshold {
      filter          = "metric.type=\"compute.googleapis.com/
                         instance/cpu/utilization\""
      comparison      = "COMPARISON_GT"
      duration        = "60s"
      threshold_value = 0.8

      aggregations {
        alignment_period   = "60s"
        per_series_aligner = "ALIGN_MEAN"
      }
    }
  }

  notification_channels = [google_monitoring_notification_
                           channel.email.id]

  combiner = "OR"
  enabled  = true
}
```

This example demonstrates an alert policy that continuously monitors the average CPU utilization of GCE instances over 60-second intervals. If the average CPU utilization for any instance exceeds 80% for a minute, an alert will be triggered and a notification sent through the designated channel.

Integrating Auditing and Monitoring

Combining auditing and monitoring provides a comprehensive view of your cloud environment. While auditing focuses on tracking changes and access to resources, monitoring ensures that you stay informed about the performance and health of those resources. By using Terraform to automate the setup of both auditing and monitoring tools, you can maintain a consistent and scalable approach to managing your cloud environment.

Summary

As we wrap up this chapter, let's reflect on the key strategies and Terraform practices we've covered to build a secure and resilient cloud environment:

- **Managing Secrets**: We've explored how to safeguard sensitive information like API keys and passwords using Terraform. By leveraging tools like Google Secret Manager, you can securely store and access secrets, ensuring that your credentials are always protected.

- **Encryption**: We delved into the importance of encryption in safeguarding your data. You've learned how to implement Google-managed and customer-managed encryption keys (GMEK and CMEK) through Terraform, keeping your data locked down and managing secret versions effectively.

- **Handling Sensitive Data with Variables**: You now know how to securely manage sensitive information using Terraform variables. We covered best practices for keeping variable values secure and safely passing data to your applications.

- **Access Control**: We know how to enhance security with Identity and Access Management and setting up precise access controls.

- **Secure Remote State Management**: We emphasised the importance of protecting your Terraform state files. You've learned how to manage remote state securely, set up appropriate access controls, and safeguard your critical infrastructure data.

- **Disaster Recovery and Regular Backups**: We discussed strategies for preparing for disasters with Terraform, including setting up automated backups and disaster recovery environments. These practices ensure that your data remains safe and your infrastructure remains resilient.

- **Auditing, Monitoring, and Alerting**: Finally, we covered how to implement comprehensive auditing and monitoring strategies. You learned how to use Terraform to set up Cloud Audit Logs, configure alerts for critical metrics, and monitor your resources to catch issues before they escalate.

By implementing these practices with Terraform, you're well-equipped to build a cloud environment that is both secure and resilient, ready to handle any challenges that come your way.

CHAPTER 6

Testing and Automation

You've now mastered the essentials of Terraform and are equipped to provision and manage infrastructure, whether it's on-premises or in the cloud. That's a major milestone!

But hold on a second. Between development and production lies the critical step of testing. Just as in traditional development, testing is a crucial part of infrastructure as code (IaC).

In this chapter, we will dive into various testing strategies, explore how to integrate our code with DevOps tools, and automate the process for efficiency. Let's explore how to navigate this challenging landscape effectively.

Testing

When tasked with testing, our minds often jump to advanced tools and complex strategies. However, the cornerstone of effective testing is rooted in the basics. Before delving into intricate testing methodologies, it's crucial to focus on foundational checks to ensure your Terraform configurations are both syntactically correct and logically sound.

It's frequently not the grand challenges that pose the greatest risk but rather the seemingly minor and often overlooked details that can trip us up. This is why placing emphasis on syntax checking and configuration validation is paramount.

© Ivy Wang 2024
I. Wang, *Terraform Made Easy*, https://doi.org/10.1007/979-8-8688-1010-7_6

Initial Testing and Validation

Terraform offers a suite of commands designed for initial validation and syntax checking, which are essential for maintaining the integrity of your configurations:

> `terraform fmt`: This command automatically formats your Terraform configuration files. By adhering to a consistent style, it enhances readability and reduces the likelihood of syntax errors, making it easier for you and your team to review and maintain the code.

> `terraform validate`: Running this command checks the syntax and structure of your Terraform files, ensuring that they are valid and internally consistent. This validation process does not interact with remote systems but rather performs a comprehensive assessment of the local configuration, identifying any issues before they become problematic.

> `terraform plan`: This command provides a preview of the changes that Terraform will apply to your infrastructure. By reviewing this plan, you can anticipate and address potential issues before executing the changes, thereby minimizing the risk of unexpected outcomes.

By prioritizing these basic yet essential steps, you lay a solid foundation for more advanced testing.

Testing Tools and Frameworks

Testing your Terraform code is essential for maintaining infrastructure that is not only reliable but also secure and efficient. Proper testing helps prevent costly errors and ensures your infrastructure as code (IaC) adheres to organizational standards and best practices. In this guide, we'll focus on popular tools and frameworks that streamline Terraform testing. Instead of diving deeply into specific testing methodologies, we'll explore tools like TFLint and Checkov, using real-world examples to illustrate their strengths and use cases. This will help you make informed decisions about which tools to integrate into your development workflow.

TFLint

TFLint is a powerful linter specifically designed for Terraform. It helps catch potential issues such as syntax errors, improper resource usage, and violations of best practices early in the development process, saving time and reducing deployment risks. It aims to catch mistakes early in the development process.

TFLint's Capabilities

The following are TFLint's main features.

Syntax Error Detection

If you accidentally omit a closing brace or make a typo in a resource name, TFLint will immediately flag the error. For instance, if you have a missing closing brace in a `resource` block, TFLint will point it out, allowing you to correct the mistake before it leads to a failed `terraform plan` or `terraform apply`.

Unused Variables

TFLint can identify variables declared in your Terraform configuration that are not used anywhere in your code. For example, if you declare a variable for `instance_type` but never reference it, TFLint will prompt you to either remove the unused variable or integrate it into your configuration. This helps maintain a clean, understandable codebase and reduces confusion about the purpose of these variables.

Enforcing Best Practices

TFLint enforces best practices by identifying configurations that may not adhere to recommended guidelines. For example, if you're using an outdated AWS resource type or missing a required attribute (such as an AMI ID in an `aws_instance` resource), TFLint will warn you, helping you maintain a compliant and efficient infrastructure.

It also ensures consistency in resource naming conventions. TFLint can alert you if a resource name does not match the expected pattern, ensuring that all resources are named consistently across your codebase.

Pre-commit Hook Integration

To ensure code quality before any changes are committed, you can use `tflint` as a pre-commit hook. This means that every time you attempt to commit code, `tflint` will automatically run and check for any issues. Only clean, error-free code will be allowed to proceed to the version control system, enforcing high standards across the team.

For example, when you use `tflint` to check a storage bucket configuration file with a deliberate mistake, you may see the output as follows:

```
2 issues found:

[ERROR] google_storage_bucket.example: Logging configuration
is missing
```

Bucket should have a logging block to comply with best practices.

[WARNING] google_storage_bucket.example: Resource name does not match the expected pattern
  Resource name "example-bucket" does not follow the
  convention: ^[a-z0-9-]+$

With the specific error and clear explanation, you can fix or improve your code quickly. In this case, the revised code may look like this:

```
provider "google" {
  project = "terraform-made-easy"
  region  = "us-west1"
}

resource "google_storage_bucket" "example" {
  name          = "example-bucket-dev"
  location      = "US"
  force_destroy = true

  lifecycle_rule {
    action {
      type = "Delete"
    }
    condition {
      age = 365
    }
  }

  logging {
    log_bucket        = "logging-bucket"
    log_object_prefix = "example-bucket/"
  }
}
```

Checkov

Checkov is an open-source tool designed to help you secure your IaC configurations. Whether you're working with Terraform, CloudFormation, Kubernetes, or other IaC frameworks, Checkov scans your code to identify potential misconfigurations and vulnerabilities before they reach production. It supports a range of cloud providers including AWS, Azure, and Google Cloud, ensuring that your infrastructure remains secure and compliant.

Checkov's Capabilities

Extensive Policy Library

Checkov comes with a rich set of built-in policies that cover a broad spectrum of security best practices and compliance standards. These policies are crafted to catch common security issues such as open security groups, unencrypted data storage, and missing logging configurations. For example, if your Terraform script includes a Google Cloud Storage bucket without encryption, Checkov will flag this as a security risk, helping you ensure sensitive data is adequately protected.

Custom Policy Creation

Need policies that are tailored to your organization's specific needs? Checkov lets you create custom policies to enforce your internal guidelines or regulatory requirements. For instance, if your company requires that all EC2 instances must be tagged with `Environment` and `Owner`, you can design a custom Checkov policy to ensure that every instance in your Terraform code meets this standard.

Detailed Reporting and Remediation Guidance

When Checkov identifies issues, it provides detailed reports along with specific guidance on how to resolve them. This helps developers quickly understand and address security vulnerabilities or compliance issues. For example, Checkov might flag issues as following:

```
Check: CKV_GCP_63: "Bucket should not log to itself" FAILED for
resource: google_storage_bucket.buckets[0] File: /tf.json:0-0
Guide: https://docs.prismacloud.io/en/enterprise-edition/
policy-reference/google-cloud-policies/google-cloud-storage-
gcs-policies/bc-gcp-logging-3
```

```
Check: CKV_GCP_29: "Ensure that Cloud Storage buckets have
uniform bucket-level access enabled" FAILED for resource:
google_storage_bucket.buckets[0] File: /tf.json:0-0 Guide:
https://docs.prismacloud.io/en/enterprise-edition/policy-reference/
google-cloud-policies/google-cloud-storage-gcs-policies/bc-gcp-gcs-2
```

Integration with CI/CD Pipelines

Checkov seamlessly integrates with CI/CD pipelines, automating the process of scanning IaC configurations during development. For instance, by integrating Checkov with GitHub Actions, you can automatically scan every pull request for security and compliance issues before merging, ensuring that only secure and compliant code is deployed to production.

Example: Testing for AWS Terraform Configuration

Suppose the AWS configuration file looks like this:

```
# main.tf
provider "aws" {
  region = "us-east-1"
}
```

```
resource "aws_s3_bucket" "my_bucket" {
  bucket = "my-unique-bucket-name"
  acl    = "private"
}

resource "aws_security_group" "my_sg" {
  name        = "my_security_group"
  description = "Allow inbound traffic"

  ingress {
    from_port   = 80
    to_port     = 80
    protocol    = "tcp"
    cidr_blocks = ["0.0.0.0/0"]
  }
}

resource "aws_rds_instance" "my_db" {
  instance_class    = "db.t2.micro"
  allocated_storage = 20
  engine   = "mysql"
  username = "admin"
  password = "password123"
}
```

To ensure that this configuration adheres to security best practices, you can use Checkov to scan it:

```
checkov -d /path/to/terraform/main.tf
```

The output may look like this:

```
Check: CKV_AWS_1: "Ensure S3 bucket is not publicly accessible"
  FAIL: aws_s3_bucket.my_bucket: Bucket should have "block_
  public_acls" set to true
```

Check: CKV_AWS_2: "Ensure security group doesn't allow unrestricted access"
  FAIL: aws_security_group.my_sg: Security group allows unrestricted access on port 80

Check: CKV_AWS_3: "Ensure RDS instance is not publicly accessible"
  FAIL: aws_rds_instance.my_db: RDS instance should have "publicly_accessible" set to false

In this example, CKV_AWS_1 checks if the S3 bucket is configured to block public ACLs. CKV_AWS_2 ensures that security groups do not allow unrestricted access, and CKV_AWS_3 ensures that the RDS instance is not publicly accessible to avoid potential security risks.

Example: Customizing Checkov Policies

Sometimes, your organization might have specific requirements that aren't covered by the default checks. For instance, you might want to ensure that all AWS S3 buckets have a specific tag.

First, you need to create a custom Checkov policy in Python to ensure that all AWS S3 buckets have a specific tag.

```python
# custom_check.py

from checkov.common.models.enums import CheckType
from checkov.common.checks.base_check import BaseCheck
from checkov.common.models.enums import CheckResult

class CheckS3BucketTags(BaseCheck):
    def __init__(self):
        name = "Ensure S3 buckets have the 'Environment' tag"
        id = "CUSTOM_S3_TAG_CHECK"
        supported_resources = ["aws_s3_bucket"]
```

```
        categories = [CheckType.TAG]
        super().__init__(name=name, id=id, supported_
        resources=supported_resources, categories=categories)

    def scan_resource_conf(self, conf):
        if "tags" not in conf:
            return CheckResult.FAILED
        tags = conf["tags"]
        if tags.get("Environment") != "production":
            return CheckResult.FAILED
        return CheckResult.PASSED

check = CheckS3BucketTags()
```

Next, run Checkov with this custom policy:

```
checkov -d /path/to/terraform/main.tf --check-class-path /path/
to/custom_check.py
```

This custom check ensures that every AWS S3 bucket has an Environment tag with the value production. If the tag is missing or has a different value, the check will fail.

These two examples demonstrate how Checkov can be used to validate your Terraform configurations and how you can create custom policies to enforce specific standards.

Example: Integrating Checkov with Jenkins

To automate Checkov scans as part of your CI/CD pipeline in Jenkins, you can use the following Jenkins Pipeline script:

```
pipeline {
    agent any

    stages {
        stage('Checkout') {
```

```
        steps {
            checkout scm
        }
    }
    stage('Set up Python and Checkov') {
        steps {
            script {
                // Set up Python and install Checkov
                sh 'python3 -m venv venv'
                sh '. venv/bin/activate'
                sh 'pip install checkov'
            }
        }
    }
    stage('Run Checkov') {
        steps {
            script {
                // Run Checkov
                sh 'checkov -d . --quiet'
            }
        }
    }
}
post {
    always {
        // Archive Checkov reports or logs if needed
        archiveArtifacts artifacts: '**/checkov.log',
        allowEmptyArchive: true
    }
}
}
```

Don't be afraid of the Jenkinsfile. Let's break it down step-by-step.

The `checkout scm` step retrieves your code from the repository, followed by `Set up Python and Checkov`, which creates a Python virtual environment, activates it, and installs Checkov. The `Run Checkov` step then executes the Checkov scan on the current directory while suppressing verbose output. Finally, the `Archive Checkov Logs` step stores the Checkov logs as artifacts for future reference.

This example demonstrates a basic setup for integrating Checkov into your CI/CD pipelines to validate your IaC for security and compliance issues as part of your automated workflows.

By incorporating Checkov into your pipeline, every code change is automatically scanned for misconfigurations and vulnerabilities, ensuring a proactive approach to security. For instance, Checkov can detect common issues such as open security groups, unencrypted storage, and missing logging configurations.

In addition to its extensive library of built-in rules, Checkov allows the creation of custom policies tailored to your organization's specific requirements. This flexibility ensures your code adheres to both internal guidelines and external regulatory standards.

Early integration of Checkov in the development lifecycle helps flag potential risks before they reach production. This not only reduces the likelihood of security incidents but minimizes the costs and effort associated with post-deployment remediation. With Checkov, your CI/CD workflows become a critical line of defense, ensuring secure and compliant IaC deployments.

Terratest

Terratest is a powerful open-source framework designed to test your IaC configurations, ensuring that your infrastructure is reliable, scalable, and performs as expected. By enabling you to write automated tests for your Terraform configurations, Terratest ensures that your infrastructure deployment is validated in a real cloud environment rather than just through static code analysis.

Terratest stands out because it provisions real infrastructure in your cloud environment for testing, uncovering issues that static analysis might miss. This hands-on approach helps validate not only the code but also the real-world behavior of your infrastructure.

Unlike some IaC testing tools that perform static analysis, Terratest provides real infrastructure in your cloud environment for testing. This approach helps uncover issues that might not be detected through code analysis alone.

Example: Modules Testing

Terratest is excellent for verifying the functionality of Terraform modules. For example, if you have a Terraform module that provisions a Google Cloud Platform (GCP) VPC network, you can use Terratest to do the following:

Provision the Network: Deploy the VPC and its associated resources (like subnets and routes) in a real GCP environment.

Verify Properties: Check that the VPC has the expected IP CIDR block, subnet configurations, and other properties. For instance, you can test that the subnet created has the correct CIDR range and is properly associated with the VPC.

Here's a Go code example using Terratest to perform these tasks:

```
package test

import (
  "testing"
  "github.com/gruntwork-io/terratest/modules/terraform"
```

```go
    "github.com/stretchr/testify/assert"
)

func TestVpcModule(t *testing.T) {
  t.Parallel() // Run tests in parallel to speed up the
  test suite

  // Define Terraform options for the test
  terraformOptions := &terraform.Options{
    TerraformDir: "../examples/vpc", // Directory containing
    Terraform configuration files
    Vars: map[string]interface{}{
      "region": "us-central1", // Variable for the
      region to use
    },
    NoColor: true, // Disable color output for easier
    reading of logs
  }

  // Ensure resources are cleaned up after tests
  defer terraform.Destroy(t, terraformOptions)

  // Initialize and apply Terraform configuration
  terraform.InitAndApply(t, terraformOptions)

  // Retrieve the output from the Terraform configuration
  vpcId := terraform.Output(t, terraformOptions, "vpc_id")
  assert.NotEmpty(t, vpcId, "VPC ID should not be empty")

  // Example of additional property checks
  // Check if the VPC has the correct CIDR block
  expectedCidrBlock := "10.0.0.0/16"
  actualCidrBlock := terraform.Output(t, terraformOptions,
  "vpc_cidr_block")
```

```
assert.Equal(t, expectedCidrBlock, actualCidrBlock, "VPC CIDR
block does not match expected value")

// Check if the subnet is associated with the VPC
subnetId := terraform.Output(t, terraformOptions, "subnet_id")
assert.NotEmpty(t, subnetId, "Subnet ID should not be empty")

//  Check other properties as needed

}
```

Example: End-to-End Infrastructure Testing

For comprehensive testing of an entire infrastructure setup, Terratest is ideal. Suppose you're deploying a multitier application on AWS, involving VPCs, subnets, and security groups:

> **Deploy Resources**: Use Terratest to apply your Terraform configurations.
>
> **Verify Configuration**: After deployment, ensure that each component is created as expected and that they work together properly. Key aspects to verify include the following:
>
> - **Resource Creation**: Confirm that all components like VPCs, subnets, and security groups are correctly provisioned.
>
> - **Security Group Rules**: Check that security groups have the correct inbound and outbound rules.
>
> - **Application Accessibility**: Ensure that your application's load balancer or any other access points are functioning as intended.

Here's a practical example using Terratest to test a multitier application deployment on AWS:

```go
func TestMultiTierDeployment(t *testing.T) {
  t.Parallel()

  // Define options for the Terraform configuration
  terraformOptions := &terraform.Options{
    TerraformDir: "../examples/multi-tier", // Path to the
    Terraform configuration
    Vars: map[string]interface{}{
      "region": "us-west-1", // Specify the AWS region
    },
    NoColor: true,
  }

  // Ensure that resources are destroyed after the test
  defer terraform.Destroy(t, terraformOptions)

  // Initialize and apply the Terraform configuration
  terraform.InitAndApply(t, terraformOptions)

  // Retrieve the instance ID of a resource (e.g., an EC2
  instance)
  instanceId := terraform.Output(t, terraformOptions,
  "instance_id")
  assert.NotEmpty(t, instanceId, "Expected instance_id to be
  non-empty")

  // Additional checks
  // Example: Verify that the instance is running
  instanceStatus := getInstanceStatus(instanceId)
  assert.Equal(t, "running", instanceStatus, "Expected instance
  to be in running state")
}
```

```
// Helper function to get the status of an EC2 instance
func getInstanceStatus(instanceId string) string {
  svc := ec2.New(session.Must(session.NewSession()))
  result, err := svc.DescribeInstances(&ec2.DescribeInstancesInput{
    InstanceIds: aws.StringSlice([]string{instanceId}),
  })
  if err != nil {
    log.Fatalf("Failed to describe instance: %v", err)
  }
  return *result.Reservations[0].Instances[0].State.Name
}
```

First, the test initializes and applies the Terraform configuration located in the specified directory. This deployment provisions all necessary infrastructure components.

Next, the `terraform.Output` function is used to retrieve the output values defined in your Terraform configuration, such as the `instance_id` of an EC2 instance.

Then, the `getInstanceStatus` helper function queries AWS for the status of the instance and verifies that it is in the "running" state. You can add more checks as needed, such as validating network connectivity or load balancer health.

Example: CI/CD Pipeline Integration

Integrating Terratest into your CI/CD pipeline automates the process of validating your IaC configurations, ensuring that your infrastructure is tested for correctness and compliance as part of your build and deployment process. This integration helps catch issues early and maintains high standards for your infrastructure deployments.

Steps to Integrate Terratest with GitHub Actions

Configure the Workflow: Set up a GitHub Actions workflow to trigger Terratest after applying your Terraform code. This ensures that your tests run automatically, validating your infrastructure as part of the continuous integration and deployment process.

Verify Compliance: Use Terratest to ensure that your infrastructure meets all specified requirements and that no unintended changes have been introduced. This helps in maintaining the integrity and stability of your infrastructure.

Here's a sample GitHub Actions workflow configuration to run Terratest:

```
name: Terraform Test

on:
  push:
    branches:
      - main

jobs:
  test:
    runs-on: ubuntu-latest

    steps:
      - name: Checkout code
        uses: actions/checkout@v2

      - name: Set up Go
        uses: actions/setup-go@v2
        with:
          go-version: '1.22'

      - name: Install Terraform
        uses: hashicorp/setup-terraform@v1
```

```
with:
  terraform_version: 1.8.0
- name: Run Terratest
run: |
  go test -v ./test
```

Terratest is a robust solution for testing Terraform configurations, ensuring your infrastructure is both reliable and compliant. By incorporating Terratest into your CI/CD pipeline, you enhance the quality and stability of your deployments and maintain higher confidence in your infrastructure.

Python Scripts

While tools like Terratest (written in Go) and other specialized testing frameworks are highly popular and powerful, leveraging Python for testing Terraform configurations can offer distinct advantages. Python is known for its flexibility and rich ecosystem, which can be particularly useful for teams already using Python or those integrating with Python-based tools.

Python's extensive libraries and tools enhance its capabilities for Terraform testing and automation. For instance:

- **pytest**: A robust testing framework for writing simple as well as scalable test cases.

- **boto3**: The Amazon Web Services (AWS) SDK for Python, useful for interacting with AWS services programmatically

These libraries make Python a strong candidate for automating and extending Terraform tests. Additionally, Python's integration with various systems and APIs allows for sophisticated validation tasks and seamless connections with other services.

Example: Using pytest for an AWS EC2 Instance

Suppose you have a Terraform configuration file that provisions an AWS EC2 instance. You can write a Python script using pytest to verify that the instance is correctly provisioned and configured.

Here is an example Python test script:

```python
import boto3  # Connects to AWS
import pytest

# Initialize a boto3 client
ec2 = boto3.client('ec2', region_name='us-central-1')

def test_ec2_instance():
    # Retrieve the list of instances
    response = ec2.describe_instances(Filters=[
        {
            'Name': 'instance-type',
            'Values': ['t2.micro']
        }
    ])
    # Check if at least one instance is found
    instances = [i for r in response['Reservations'] for i in
                 r['Instances']]
    assert len(instances) > 0, "No EC2 instances found with the
    specified type"

    # Check instance details
    instance = instances[0]
    assert instance['InstanceType'] == 't2.micro', "Instance
    type is not t2.micro"

if __name__ == "__main__":
    pytest.main()
```

Example: Using Python to Validate Terraform Outputs for VPC Subnetwork

Validating Terraform outputs for VPC subnetwork configurations with Python involves fetching and verifying the outputs produced by Terraform after deployment. This ensures your infrastructure meets your requirements, such as subnet CIDR blocks, availability zones, and tags.

First, define your terraform configuration and ensure it contains appropriate output variables. Here is a `main.tf` example:

```
provider "google" {
  region = "us-east1"
}

resource "google_compute_network" "my_vpc" {
  cidr_block = "10.0.0.0/24"
}

resource "google_compute_subnetwork" "my_subnet" {
name = "my-subnet"
network = google_compute_network.my_vpc.id ip_cidr_range =
          "10.0.1.0/24"
region = "us-east1" }

output "subnet_id" {
  value = aws_subnet.my_subnet.id
}

output "subnet_cidr_block" {
  value = aws_subnet.my_subnet.cidr_block
}

output "subnet_availability_zone" {
  value = aws_subnet.my_subnet.availability_zone
}
```

231

Next, write a Python script to validate these outputs. This script uses the subprocess module to run Terraform commands and json to parse the output. The pytest framework is used for testing.

The following is a Python script example:

```python
import subprocess
import json
import pytest

def get_terraform_output():
    """Run terraform output command and return JSON parsed
    output."""
    result = subprocess.run(['terraform', 'output', '-json'],
capture_output=True, text=True)
    if result.returncode != 0:
        raise Exception(f"Terraform output command failed with
        error: {result.stderr}")
    return json.loads(result.stdout)

def test_subnet_id():
    """Test to validate the subnet ID output."""
    outputs = get_terraform_output()
    subnet_id = outputs.get('subnet_id', {}).get('value')
    assert subnet_id is not None, "Subnet ID output is missing"
    assert isinstance(subnet_id, str) and len(subnet_id) > 0,
    "Subnet ID output is invalid"

def test_subnet_cidr_block():
    """Test to validate the subnet CIDR block output."""
    outputs = get_terraform_output()
    subnet_cidr_block = outputs.get('subnet_cidr_block', {}).
    get('value')
    assert subnet_cidr_block == "10.0.1.0/24", "Subnet CIDR
    block output is incorrect"
```

```python
def test_subnet_availability_zone():
    """Test to validate the subnet availability zone output."""
    outputs = get_terraform_output()
    subnet_availability_zone = outputs.get('subnet_
    availability_zone', {}).get('value')
    assert subnet_availability_zone == "us-west-2a", "Subnet
    availability zone output is incorrect"

if __name__ == "__main__":
    pytest.main()
```

Example: Integrating Python Tests into CI/CD Pipelines

You can integrate Python tests into your CI/CD pipelines to automate the validation of your Terraform configurations. For example, in a GitHub Actions workflow:

```yaml
name: Terraform and Python Test

on:
  push:
    branches:
      - main

jobs:
  test:
    runs-on: ubuntu-latest

    steps:
      - name: Checkout code
        uses: actions/checkout@v2

      - name: Set up Python
        uses: actions/setup-python@v2
        with:
```

```
      python-version: '3.10'
 - name: Install dependencies
   run: |
     pip install boto3 pytest
 - name: Run Terraform
   run: |
     terraform init
     terraform apply -auto-approve
 - name: Run Python Tests
   run: |
     pytest
```

In this example, the workflow is quite straightforward. It configures the Python environment and then installs dependencies. Next, it applies Terraform configurations and executes the Python test scripts.

Automation

In the final section of this book, we focus on automation—a crucial aspect that will enhance your Terraform skills, making your infrastructure management both more efficient and effective. By this point, you are well-versed in the intricacies of Terraform and prepared to harness its full potential. You've already encountered some automation examples in the "Testing" section, laying the groundwork for deeper exploration into automating infrastructure management.

Integrating Terraform with CI/CD Pipelines

Automation through continuous integration/continuous deployment (CI/CD) pipelines is a transformative approach to managing infrastructure. By incorporating Terraform into your CI/CD workflow, you can automate the provisioning and management of infrastructure, ensuring that deployments are consistent, repeatable, and reliable. In a typical CI/CD workflow, code changes trigger automated build and deployment processes. With Terraform, this means that every change committed to your version control system initiates a series of automated actions: Terraform plans the infrastructure changes, applies those changes, and deploys them in a controlled and predictable manner. This integration not only accelerates the deployment cycle but also minimizes the risk of human error, enhancing overall infrastructure stability and adherence to best practices.

Popular CI/CD Tools for Terraform Integration

To automate Terraform deployments, consider using one of the following popular CI/CD tools:

- **GitHub Actions**: A built-in automation tool within GitHub that lets you define workflows in YAML. It's ideal for automating Terraform tasks such as initialization, validation, planning, and applying changes directly from your repository.

- **GitLab CI**: Integrated into GitLab, this tool allows you to manage CI/CD pipelines with `.gitlab-ci.yml` files. It supports stages for Terraform operations and provides a complete environment for handling development lifecycle tasks.

- **Jenkins**: A versatile, open-source automation server with extensive plugin support. Jenkins pipelines can be configured to handle Terraform operations, offering flexibility for various infrastructure automation needs.

Examples with Popular CI/CD Tools

These are some examples of tools you can use.

Terraform with GitHub Actions

First, you need to create and define a workflow in the `.github/workflows/terraform.yml` file.

The following is an example of the workflow. The Terraform workflow is set up to automatically run whenever there are changes to the `main` branch, whether through direct pushes or pull requests. This workflow helps manage Terraform infrastructure as code on an Ubuntu-latest GitHub-hosted runner.

```
name: Terraform

on:
  push:
    branches:
      - main
  pull_request:
    branches:
      - main

jobs:
  terraform:
    name: Terraform
    runs-on: ubuntu-latest
    steps:
    - name: Checkout code
      uses: actions/checkout@v3

    - name: Set up Terraform
      uses: hashicorp/setup-terraform@v2
```

```
    with:
      terraform_version: 1.8.0

- name: Terraform Init
  run: terraform init

- name: Terraform Validate
  run: terraform validate

- name: Terraform Plan
  run: terraform plan

- name: Terraform Apply
  env:
    TF_VAR_my_secret: ${{ secrets.MY_SECRET }}
  run: terraform apply -auto-approve
```

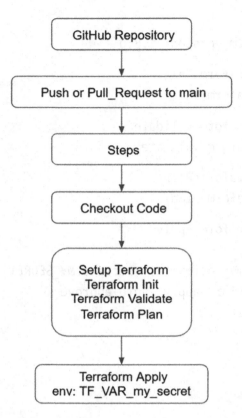

Figure 6-1. *Workflow Illustration Using GitHub Actions for CI/CD*

Trigger

The workflow starts when there are changes (pushes or pull requests) to
the main branch. This means any updates to the Terraform configuration
will automatically trigger the workflow.

Fetch Code

The actions/checkout@v3 action fetches the code from the GitHub
repository. This ensures that the Terraform configuration files are available
on the GitHub Actions runner.

Set up Terraform

The `hashicorp/setup-terraform@v2` action installs the specified version of Terraform (version 1.8.0 in this case). This step ensures that Terraform is ready to manage your infrastructure and makes the necessary Terraform binaries available for execution.

Terraform Workflow Steps

These are the steps:

1. **Initialization**: `terraform init` sets up the Terraform configuration, downloading any necessary provider and back-end configuration files.

2. **Validation**: `terraform validate` checks that the configuration is correct and follows best practices. This prevents errors before making changes.

3. **Plan**: `terraform plan` shows what changes Terraform intends to make, without applying them. It provides a preview so that you can review and approve the changes before they go live.

4. **Apply**: `terraform apply` applies the planned changes to the live infrastructure. The `-auto-approve` flag skips the approval prompt, assuming the changes have already been reviewed. The `TF_VAR_my_secret` environment variable ensures that sensitive information (like API keys or database passwords) isn't hard-coded in the source code.

Terraform with GitLab CI

Here is an example of using `.gitlab-ci.yml` for pipeline configuration and automation.

This GitLab CI configuration automates the process of managing infrastructure using Terraform. The pipeline consists of three stages: `validate`, `plan`, and `apply`. Each stage is designed to perform specific tasks.

```
stages:
  - validate
  - plan
  - apply

variables:
  TF_VERSION: 1.4.0
  TF_BACKEND_BUCKET: "my-terraform-state"
  TF_BACKEND_KEY: "terraform/state"
  TF_BACKEND_REGION: "us-east-1"

before_script:
  - apk add --no-cache curl git
  - curl -LO https://releases.hashicorp.com/terraform/${TF_
    VERSION}/terraform_${TF_VERSION}_linux_amd64.zip
  - unzip terraform_${TF_VERSION}_linux_amd64.zip
  - mv terraform /usr/local/bin/
  - terraform --version

validate:
  stage: validate
  script:
    - terraform init -backend-config="bucket=${TF_BACKEND_
      BUCKET}" -backend-config="key=${TF_BACKEND_KEY}"
      -backend-config="region=${TF_BACKEND_REGION}"
    - terraform validate
```

```
plan:
  stage: plan
  script:
    - terraform plan
  artifacts:
    paths:
      - plan.out

apply:
  stage: apply
  script:
    - terraform apply -auto-approve
  only:
    - main
```

The `validate` stage checks if the Terraform configuration is syntactically correct and can be parsed successfully. It initializes Terraform with the backend configuration pointing to an S3 bucket (`TF_BACKEND_BUCKET`), key (`TF_BACKEND_KEY`), and region (`TF_BACKEND_REGION`). After initialization, it performs a validation with `terraform validate` to ensure there are no errors in the configuration.

The `plan` stage generates an execution plan that shows what changes Terraform intends to make to the infrastructure. It runs `terraform plan`, which details the changes and outputs them to a file named `plan.out`. This output is used in the next stage to apply the changes automatically.

The `apply` stage automatically applies the planned changes to the infrastructure using `terraform apply -auto-approve`. This stage runs only when changes are pushed to the `main` branch, ensuring that the changes are applied only when explicitly approved by the main branch updates. This setup allows for fully automated management of infrastructure changes from planning to deployment.

Terraform with Jenkins

You can use Jenkins pipeline to automate infrastructure management using Terraform, too.

First, you need to set up a Jenkins pipeline with a Jenkinsfile.

```
pipeline {
    agent any
    environment {
        TF_VERSION = '1.8.0'
        TF_BUCKET = 'my-terraform-state'
        TF_KEY = 'terraform/state'
        TF_REGION = 'us-east-1'
    }
    stages {
        stage('Checkout') {
            steps {
                git 'https://github.com/your-repo/terraform-
                code.git'
            }
        }
        stage('Install Terraform') {
            steps {
                sh '''
                curl -LO https://releases.hashicorp.com/terraform/$
                {TF_VERSION}/terraform_${TF_VERSION}_linux_
                amd64.zip
                unzip terraform_${TF_VERSION}_linux_amd64.zip
                sudo mv terraform /usr/local/bin/
                terraform --version
                '''
            }
        }
```

```
    stage('Terraform Init') {
        steps {
            sh '''
            terraform init \
              -backend-config="bucket=${TF_BUCKET}" \
              -backend-config="key=${TF_KEY}" \
              -backend-config="region=${TF_REGION}"
            '''
        }
    }
    stage('Terraform Validate') {
        steps {
            sh 'terraform validate'
        }
    }
    stage('Terraform Plan') {
        steps {
            sh 'terraform plan'
        }
    }
    stage('Terraform Apply') {
        steps {
            input 'Approve Terraform Apply?'
            sh 'terraform apply -auto-approve'
        }
    }
}
post {
    always {
```

```
            archiveArtifacts artifacts: 'terraform.tfstate',
            allowEmptyArchive: true
        }
    }
}
```

The stages are quite similar with the Github Actions. But in this case, the `apply` action and `post` action are different.

The pipeline waits for manual approval before applying the planned changes using `terraform apply -auto-approve`. This ensures that changes are only made when explicitly approved.

After each run, the pipeline archives the Terraform state file (`terraform.tfstate`) to keep a history of the state files.

Now, you have seen several examples so far. Each CI/CD tool offers a method to seamlessly integrate Terraform into automation workflows, enhancing efficiency and consistency in infrastructure management. You can customize the pipeline configuration to suit your specific requirements and security practices. Additionally, consider incorporating further steps such as testing and rollback procedures to ensure robustness and reliability in your deployment processes.

Summary

Congratulations on completing this book! In this chapter, we delved into testing and automation, covering various popular tools and frameworks such as TFLint, Checkov, Terratest, and Python scripts. Each tool offers unique features, advantages, and ideal use cases, allowing you to choose the best approach for your specific needs.

We also explored three leading CI/CD tools for automation, providing insights into how to read and construct your own workflows. Terraform made a lot of things easy!

In the end, I want to say that experience in testing and automation is all about continuous improvement. It's okay to make mistakes along the way; the mistakes and errors are valuable learning opportunities that help us grow and get better at what we do. The key is to embrace a mindset of experimentation and iteration—constantly refining and optimizing your processes. By doing so, you not only build better solutions but also become more adaptable and resilient in the face of challenges. So, keep pushing yourself to learn, experiment, and practice!

Further Resources

The following are where you can learn more about Terraform:

- ***Terraform in Action* by Scott Winkler:**

  https://www.manning.com/books/terraform-in-action

- ***Terraform Cookbook* by Mikael Krief:**

  https://www.packtpub.com/en-us/product/terraform-cookbook-9781804616420?srsltid=Afm
  BOookyxNZ_5Onkj1EWo57j8RFsKydeyh9w7soL9hkLl
  aHw7dSrnzv

- **Terraform: Up & Running by Yevgeniy Brikman:**

  https://www.oreilly.com/library/view/terraform-up-and/9781098116736/

- **Terraform Provider for Google Cloud Documentation:**

  https://cloud.google.com/docs/terraform

- **Terraform Documentation:**

  https://developer.hashicorp.com/terraform/docs

- **HashiCorp Terraform GitHub Repository:**

  https://github.com/hashicorp/terraform

© Ivy Wang 2024
I. Wang, *Terraform Made Easy*, https://doi.org/10.1007/979-8-8688-1010-7

- **Terraform-google-examples:**

  https://github.com/GoogleCloudPlatform/
  terraform-google-examples

- **terraform-google-modules:**

  https://github.com/terraform-google-modules

Index

© Ivy Wang 2024
I. Wang, *Terraform Made Easy*, https://doi.org/10.1007/979-8-8688-1010-7